CROCHET FOR TOTS

CROCHET FOR TOTS

20 FRESH AND FUN DESIGNS

Nancy Queen

Martingale®
& COMPANY

DEDICATION

*To Hadley, for providing endless inspiration
and joy that I bring to my work.*

*To my husband, Ben, for his support
and encouragement.*

*To my parents, Virginia and John,
who passed on their love for handcrafts.*

CREDITS

President	Nancy J. Martin
CEO	Daniel J. Martin
Publisher	Jane Hamada
Editorial Director	Mary V. Green
Managing Editor	Tina Cook
Technical Editor	Ursula Reikes
Copy Editor	Liz McGehee
Design Director	Stan Green
Illustrator	Robin Strobel
Cover and Text Designer	Regina Girard
Fashion Photographer	John Hamel
Studio Photographer	Brent Kane

Crochet for Tots: 20 Fresh and Fun Designs
© 2003 by Nancy Queen

Martingale & Company
20205 144th Avenue NE
Woodinville, WA 98072-8478 USA
www.martingale-pub.com

Printed in China
08 07 06 05 04 03   8 7 6 5 4 3 2 1

MISSION STATEMENT

*Dedicated to providing quality products
and service to inspire creativity.*

Library of Congress Cataloging-in-Publication Data
Queen, Nancy.
    Crochet for tots : 20 fresh and fun designs / Nancy Queen.
        p. cm.
        ISBN 1-56477-457-0
    1. Crocheting—Patterns. 2. Infants' clothing.
3. Children's clothing. I. Title.
    TT825 .Q52 2003
    746.43'40432—dc21

                                                    2002154144

CONTENTS

INTRODUCTION

Crochet is finding new fans among all age groups. It's a great way to relax and unwind. The sense of satisfaction you feel after completing a project is very rewarding. What better way to show your love than giving a gift you created with your own hands? As a mom on the go, I've designed fresh, updated patterns in small, easy pieces, so you can crochet anywhere, and you can complete most projects in little more than a weekend. Start crocheting for someone you love!

Nancy Queen

CROCHET BASICS

Okay, you've picked up a crochet book. Now where do you go from here? Whether you are learning for the first time or just brushing up on your techniques, this chapter will serve as an excellent reference tool. You will be amazed at what you can create using a ball of yarn, a crochet hook, and a little patience.

TOOLS OF THE TRADE

The first step in learning to crochet is identifying the necessary supplies and tools. In this section, we'll discuss yarn and the crochet hook.

YARN

All of the patterns in this book are made using DK-weight cotton yarn. I chose it because it is a great medium weight for children's clothes and, quite frankly, it works up rather quickly. I suggest that when working the patterns in this book that you use only a DK-weight yarn for best results.

If you can't find a cotton yarn in DK weight to your liking or you want to substitute something else for it, use a yarn of the same weight and same yarn blend. Otherwise, your garment may not fit as intended.

THE CROCHET HOOK

Crochet hooks come in a variety of materials and sizes. Most hooks are made of aluminum, wood, or plastic. Crochet hooks are usually about 6" long, and the diameter determines the size of the hook. American hooks are assigned a letter and number and are measured in millimeters. Patterns specify the hook size used to make the garment.

There are four main components of the crochet hook:

• Point: End used to insert the hook into the next chain or stitch

• Throat: Area that catches the yarn

• Shank: Area where stitches are worked; it determines the size of the stitches

• Thumb rest: Area where thumb rests so you can easily rotate the hook and maintain balance

Throat   Thumb rest

Point   Shank

Holding the Hook

There are two popular ways to hold a crochet hook. Practice both and use whichever one feels more comfortable.

Knife hold: Hold the hook as you would a cutting knife.

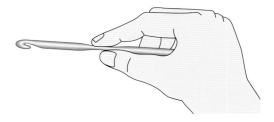

Pencil hold: Hold the hook as you would a pencil.

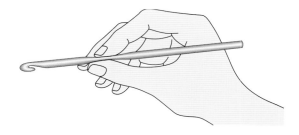

Lefties Can Crochet, Too!

All of the instructions given in this book are the same for either right-handed or left-handed crocheters. If you are learning stitches, simply place a mirror next to the book to reverse the illustration.

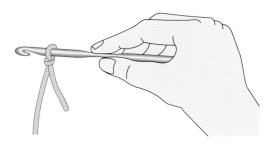

Right Hand

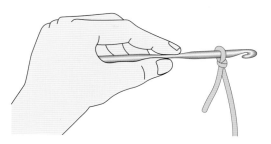

Left Hand

GETTING STARTED

Now that you know what yarn to use and what hook you need, it's time to put the two together. In this section, we'll go over the how-to basics of crochet.

MAKING THE SLIP KNOT

The slip knot is the first step to every crochet project. This step is usually not given in patterns. Leaving a 4" tail, make a loop. Insert the hook into the loop and catch the tail with the hook. Pull the yarn through the loop. Slightly tighten the loop on the hook.

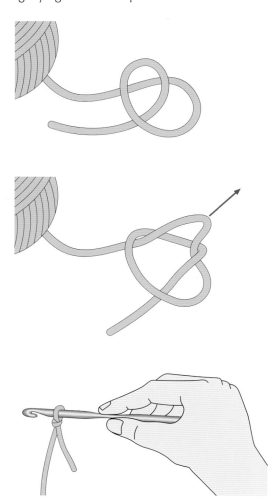

CONTROLLING THE YARN

One hand controls the crochet hook while the other hand controls the working yarn. You control the flow of the working yarn with your fingers. Weave the yarn through your fingers and maintain a comfortable tension. The most important thing to remember is that the yarn needs to flow freely through your fingers so that your stitches will be even. This method improves with practice.

LEARNING THE BASIC STITCHES

There are numerous crochet stitches. In this section, we'll describe the stitches used in this book.

Yarn Over (yo)

From the back, bring the yarn over the top of the hook to the front, catching the yarn in the throat of the hook.

Chain Stitch (ch)

To begin a chain, grasp the base of the slip knot, yarn over, and pull the yarn through the loop on the hook. You've just made your first chain stitch. Repeat this process to make a row of chain stitches. Move your thumb and finger up the chain, keeping them close to the hook. This will serve as the foundation for your first row of crochet. Be sure to work your foundation chain loosely; many beginning crocheters work it too tightly.

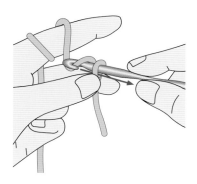

Notice there are two sides to your foundation chain. The front looks like a series of hearts or a braid. The back looks like a series of little ridges. To count the chain stitches, always count the stitches on the front side. Never count the beginning slip knot or the stitch that is on the hook. The number of chain stitches on the front side (minus the slip knot and the stitch on the hook) is known as the working chain. A pattern will state how many chain stitches to make.

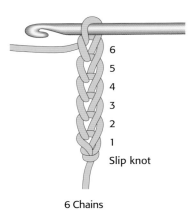

6
5
4
3
2
1
Slip knot

6 Chains

Single Crochet (sc)

Begin by making a slip knot and a foundation chain. Insert the hook into the second chain from the hook, yarn over and pull up a loop (two loops on hook), yarn over, draw through both loops on the hook. You have just made a single crochet.

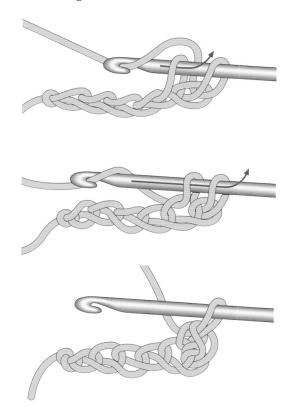

Continue working one single crochet in each chain across the row. Remember: don't crochet in the slip knot. Congratulations! You have just completed your first row of single crochet. At the end of the row, you will need to make a turning chain to add height so you can work the next row. So chain one and turn your work. Notice the row of braids or hearts in the row you just completed. This is where you will work your next row. Skip the turning chain and make one single crochet in the first single crochet. You will work this stitch going under the heart instead of through it. Continue working one single crochet in each single crochet across the row.

Half Double Crochet (hdc)

Begin by making a slip knot and a foundation chain. Yarn over, insert the hook into the third chain from the hook, yarn over and pull up a loop (three loops on hook), yarn over, draw through all three loops on the hook. You have just made a half double crochet.

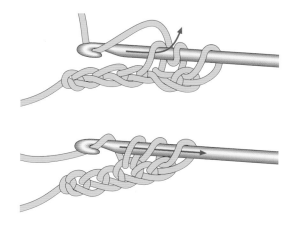

Continue working a half double crochet in each chain across. Remember: don't crochet in the slip knot. At the end of the row, make a turning chain of two and turn your work. This turning chain counts as the first stitch in the next row. This rule applies to all stitches except single crochet. Skip the first half double crochet and make one half double crochet in the next half double crochet (go under the heart to make the stitch). Continue working one half double crochet in each stitch across the row. At the end of the row, work one half double crochet in the turning chain.

Double Crochet (dc)

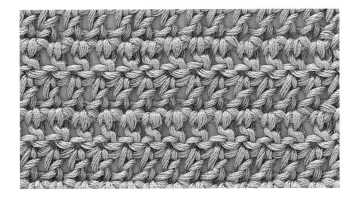

Begin by making a slip knot and a foundation chain. Yarn over, insert the hook into the fourth chain from the hook, yarn over and pull up a loop (three loops on hook). Yarn over and draw through the first two loops on the hook. Yarn over again and draw through the last two loops on the hook. You have just made a double crochet.

Continue working one double crochet in each chain across. Remember: don't crochet in the slip knot. At the end of the row, make a turning chain of three and turn your work. This turning chain counts as the first stitch in the next row. Skip the first double crochet and make one double crochet in the next double crochet (go under the heart to make the stitch). Continue working one double crochet in each stitch across the row. At the end of the row, work one double crochet in the turning chain.

Front-Post or Back-Post Double Crochet (FPdc or BPdc)

These stitches are similar to the double crochet described above, but instead of inserting the hook under the heart to make the stitch, insert the hook around the post immediately below the heart you would normally work into. For a front-post double crochet, insert the hook, from front to back, on the right side of the post. For a back-post double crochet, insert the hook from back to front on the right side of the post.

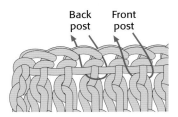

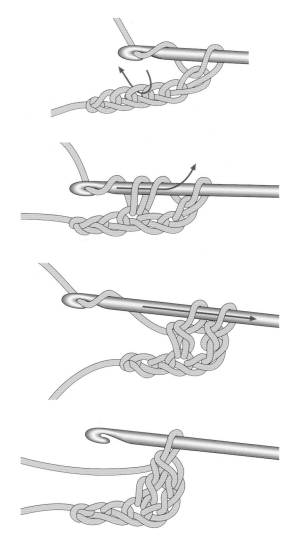

Triple Crochet (tr)

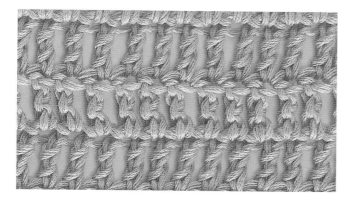

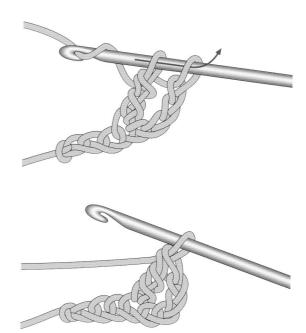

Begin by making a slip knot and a foundation chain. Yarn over, then yarn over again. Insert the hook into the fifth chain from the hook, yarn over and draw up a loop (four loops on hook). Yarn over and draw through the first two loops on the hook. Yarn over again and draw through the next two loops on the hook. Yarn over and draw through the last two loops on the hook. You have just made a triple crochet.

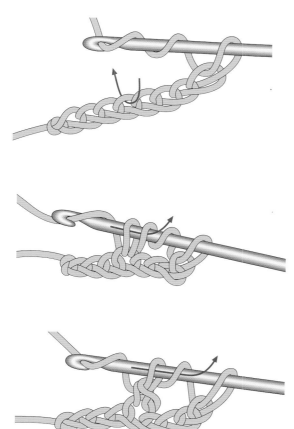

Continue working one triple crochet in each chain across. Remember: don't crochet in the slip knot. At the end of the row, make a turning chain of four and turn your work. This turning chain counts as the first stitch in the next row. Skip the first triple crochet and make one triple crochet in the next triple crochet (go under the heart to make the stitch). Continue working one triple crochet in each stitch across the row. At the end of the row, work one triple crochet in the turning chain.

Slip Stitch (sl st)

The slip stitch is primarily used to join ends of rows or rounds or to move across the row without adding height. Begin by making a slip knot and a foundation chain. Insert the hook into the second chain from the hook, yarn over, and draw through both the chain and the loop on the hook. You have just made your first slip stitch.

Free Loop (frlp)

Free loops are unworked portions of a stitch or chain. In the dresses in this book, the skirt panels are crocheted first from the waist down. The yarn is then attached to the waist, and the bodice is worked from the waist to the shoulder. Because you'll be working from the waist or the beginning of the skirt panel, you'll be working into the opposite side of the foundation chain. The unused loops of the foundation chain remaining after working the first row of single crochet into the chain are referred to as free loops in the directions.

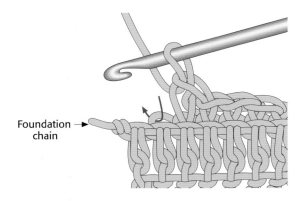

Foundation chain

CHANGING COLORS

Working in double crochet, with old color, yarn over and insert the hook into the next stitch, yarn over and draw up a loop (three loops on hook), yarn over and draw it through the next two loops on the hook. Now using the new color, loop the yarn over the hook and draw it through both loops on the hook. Continue working, using new yarn. Do not knot the ends of the yarn together. This is not necessary in crochet. Instead, weave in the yarn ends for a clean, tidy finish (see "Weaving in Yarn Ends" on page 18). This technique may also be used when joining another skein of the same color and is similar for working single, half double, and triple crochet stitches. Start the stitch with the old color, and finish the stitch with the new color.

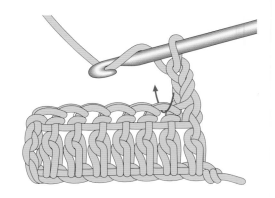

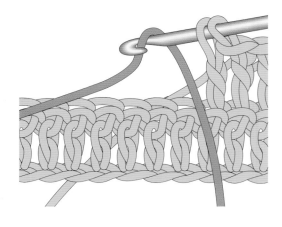

INCREASING AND DECREASING STITCHES

Increasing and decreasing stitches are techniques often used to shape a garment or make an item larger or smaller. Don't let them scare you; increasing and decreasing are quite easy.

To increase, you work two or more stitches into one stitch in the previous row. The pattern may state: work two single crochet in the next single crochet. That is an increase of one single crochet. Increasing is as simple as that.

To decrease, you work one stitch over two or three stitches in the previous row.

Decrease in Single Crochet

Insert the hook into the next stitch, yarn over and draw up a loop (two loops on hook), insert the hook into the next stitch, yarn over and draw up a loop (three loops on hook), yarn over and draw through all three loops on the hook. You have just completed a single-crochet decrease.

Decrease in Half Double Crochet

Yarn over, insert the hook into the next stitch, yarn over and draw up a loop (three loops on hook), yarn over, insert the hook into the next stitch, yarn over and draw up a loop (five loops on hook), yarn over and draw through all five loops on the hook. You have just completed a half-double-crochet decrease.

Decrease in Double Crochet

Yarn over, insert the hook into the next stitch, yarn over and draw up a loop, yarn over and draw through the first two loops on the hook (two loops remain on hook), yarn over, insert the hook into the next stitch, yarn over and pull up a loop, yarn over and draw through the next two loops on the hook (three loops remain on hook), yarn over and draw through all three loops on the hook. You have just completed a double-crochet decrease.

WORKING IN ROUNDS

This is a fun variation of crochet and is used on several of the hats in this book. Instead of working back and forth, you work around and around. You begin by making a small chain, and then work several stitches into a chain, working outward and increasing stitches as you go.

Try making a sample swatch: **Chain 2**

Round 1: Make 5 single crochet in the second chain from the hook (mark the beginning of rounds with a marker so you don't lose your place).

Round 2: Make 2 single crochet in each stitch around. You should have 10 single crochet.

Round 3: Make 2 single crochet in each stitch around. You should have 20 single crochet.

This is known as a continuous round.

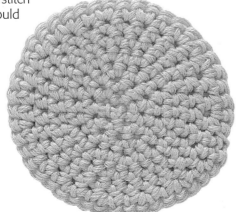

FINISHING OFF

To finish off your pieces, cut the yarn from the ball, leaving approximately a 4" tail. Yarn over and pull the tail through the loop on the hook and tighten. This is the best way to finish off all of your work.

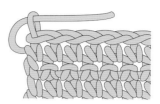

CHECKING YOUR GAUGE

There are many variables in crochet: hook size, type of yarn, the stitch itself, and how tightly or loosely you crochet. That is why you will find a gauge at the beginning of a pattern. Gauge is the number of stitches and rows per inch used to make a garment. If your gauge matches the gauge on the pattern, your finished garment will match the pattern. If your gauge is off, your finished garment will be the wrong size. It is important to check your gauge even if you are using exactly the same yarn and hook noted in the pattern. You may crochet more tightly or loosely than the designer who created the pattern.

You can check your gauge by crocheting a gauge swatch. A gauge swatch is simply a small sample of fabric crocheted in the gauge shown. To make a gauge swatch, crochet a square slightly larger than 4" using the required yarn, hook, and stitch noted in the pattern. For example, if your gauge requirements are 16 stitches and 20 rows to 4" over single crochet, make a swatch of 24 stitches and 26 rows in single crochet. This will give you an adequate area on which to measure the swatch accurately. Lay the completed swatch on a flat surface and count the number of stitches and rows in a 4" span.

If your gauge matches the gauge required, begin your project. If you have too many stitches and/or rows, try a larger hook. If you have too few stitches and/or rows, try a smaller hook. If your swatch is uneven, keep practicing your basic stitches.

Checking the gauge is often a step that beginner crocheters want to skip because they want to dive right into the project. Don't make this mistake! It is worth the extra minutes spent making an accurate gauge to ensure a proper-fitting garment.

FINISHING

JOINING SEAMS

There are several methods that you can use to join the seams of a garment.

Joining Seams with Slip Stitch

Place pieces with right sides together. Using the same yarn used to make the project, make a slip knot and *insert the hook through both edge stitches and yarn over, drawing the loop through both stitches and the loop on the hook*. Repeat from * to * across to make a seam. Finish off.

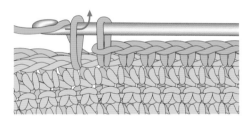

Joining Seams with Single Crochet

Place pieces with right sides together. Using the same yarn used to make the project, make a slip knot and *insert the hook through both edge stitches, yarn over and draw the loop through the stitch (two loops on hook), yarn over and draw the loop through both loops on the hook.* Repeat from * to * across to make a seam. Finish off.

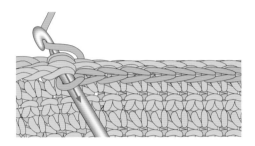

Joining Seams with Backstitch

Place pieces with right sides together. Using the same yarn used to make the project, cut a strand approximately three times the length of the pieces to be stitched. Attach the yarn to the end and insert the needle two stitches across the seam; pull through. Now insert the needle two stitches forward. Repeat this technique across the seam and finish off.

WEAVING IN YARN ENDS

This is the last thing you'll do to finish a garment. Thread a yarn needle with the yarn end. With the wrong side facing, weave the needle through several stitches in the back of the work. Clip the remaining end close to your project. Check your work from the front side to be sure the ends are not showing through.

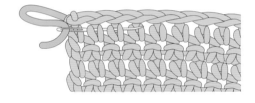

ABBREVIATIONS

beg	begin(ning)	mm	millimeter
BPdc	back-post double crochet	patt(s)	pattern(s)
ch(s)	chain(s)	rem	remaining
ch-( ) sp	chain-(number of stitches) space	rep	repeat
cont	continue, continuing	rnd(s)	round(s)
dc	double crochet	RS	right side
dec	decrease, decreasing	sc	single crochet
fp	front post	sk	skip
FPdc	front-post double crochet	sl st	slip stitch
frlp(s)	free loop	sp	space
g	gram	st(s)	stitch(es)
hdc	half-double crochet	tr	triple crochet
inc	increase, increasing	WS	wrong side
lp(s)	loop(s)	yd(s)	yard(s)
		yo	yarn over

THE PATTERN COLLECTION

These patterns are fun, fast, and easy. They include most skill levels: beginner, advanced beginner, and intermediate. If you are an experienced crocheter, you'll be pleased with the simple, yet whimsical outfits that make great gifts. If you are new to crochet and you've been practicing your crochet basics, it's now time to jump in and get started on your first pattern. Let me warn you: crochet is addictive. You'll be crocheting advanced beginner and intermediate projects in no time!

GARDEN PARTY POCKET DRESS

Celadon green and robin's-egg blue combine for a refreshing look in this A-line, knee-length party dress. Three crocheted popcorn buttons and two patch pockets complement the dress.

SIZES

Dress: 6–12M (18–24M, 2T, 3T, 4T)

Finished Chest Measurement: 22 (24, 26, 28, 30)"

MATERIALS

A 4 (4, 5, 6, 7) balls Plymouth Wildflower DK (50g, 137yds/ball; 51% cotton, 49% acrylic), Celadon Green 19

B 1 ball Plymouth Wildflower DK, Robin's Egg Blue 70

Size 5.5 mm (I/9 US) crochet hook or size needed to obtain gauge

GAUGE

16 sts and 20 rows = 4" in single crochet

Note: Dress is made by crocheting skirt panels first from the waist down, and then attaching yarn to the waist of each skirt panel and working up to the shoulder.

DRESS

SKIRT (Make 2)

With color A, ch 45 (49, 53, 57, 61).

Row 1: Work 1 sc in second ch from hook and in each ch across, ch 1, turn—44 (48, 52, 56, 60) sc.

Rows 2, 3, 4, 6, 7, 8, and 9: Work 1 sc in each sc across, ch 1, turn.

Row 5: Work 2 sc in first sc, 1 sc in each sc across, 2 sc in last sc, ch 1, turn.

Row 10: Work 2 sc in first sc, 1 sc in each sc across, 2 sc in last sc, ch 1, turn.

Rep rows 6–10 until skirt measures 8 (9, 10, 11, 12)" from beg—60 (66, 72, 78, 84) sc in last row. This is the bottom of the skirt.

BODICE BACK

With color A and RS facing, join yarn to top of skirt and sc in each frlp across (see page 16)—44 (48, 52, 56, 60) sc.

Row 1: Work 1 sc in each sc across, ch 1, turn.

Rep row 1 until back measures 6 (6¼, 6½, 6¾, 7)". Finish off.

BODICE FRONT

With color A and RS facing, join yarn to top of skirt and sc in each frlp across—44 (48, 52, 56, 60) sc.

Row 1: Work 1 sc in each sc across, ch 1, turn.

Rep row 1 until front measures 4 (4¼, 4½, 4¼, 4½)" from beg. Beg neck shaping.

NECK SHAPING

Work both sides at the same time.

Next row: Work 1 sc in first 17 (19, 20, 22, 24) sc, sk next 10 (10, 12, 12, 12) sc; with a second ball of yarn, work 1 sc in rem 17 (19, 20, 22, 24) sc.

Next 4 (4, 5, 5, 5) rows: Work across each row, dec 1 sc at neck edge—13 (15, 15, 17, 19) sc rem on each side.

Rep row 2 until front measures 6 (6¼, 6½, 6¾, 7)" from beg. Finish off.

SLEEVES (Make 2)

With color A, ch 33 (37, 37, 41, 41).

Row 1: Work 1 sc in second ch from hook and in each ch across, ch 1, turn—32 (36, 36, 40, 40) sc.

Row 2: Work 1 sc in each sc across, ch 1, turn.

Rep row 2 until sleeve measures 1½ (2, 2½, 2½, 3)" from beg. Finish off.

POCKETS (Make 2)

With color B, ch 10 (11, 12, 13, 14).

Row 1: Work 1 sc in second ch from hook and in each ch across, ch 1, turn—9 (10, 11, 12, 13) sc.

Row 2: Work 1 sc in each sc across, ch 1, turn.

Rep row 2 another 9 (10, 11, 12, 13) times. Finish off.

POPCORN BUTTONS

Find center of bodice and measure down 1¼" from neck edge. Make popcorn buttons as follows: Attach color B to front post (fp). In the same fp, work 1 sc, 5 dc, and 1 sc. Insert hook through first sc of button, sl st, and finish off. Space rem buttons 1¼" apart.

ASSEMBLY

Join shoulders: With RS of front and back together, sew 2¾ (3¼, 3½, 3¾, 4½)" from outside edge on each shoulder. Attach sleeves: Measure down 4 (4½, 4½, 5, 5)" from shoulder seam on front and back and place markers. Sew in sleeves between markers. Sew side and underarm seams.

With color A, sc 2 rows evenly around neck edge.

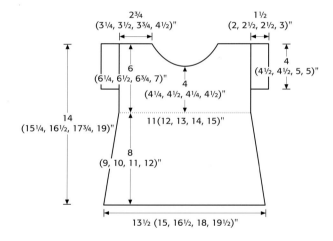

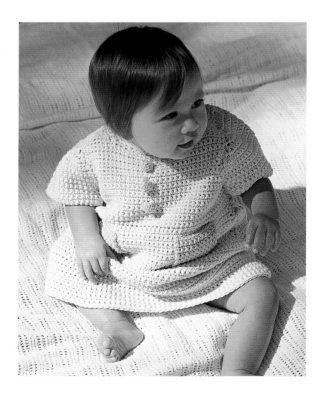

COWPOKE ROMPER

Yeee-haaa! Your favorite tyke will be ready for the ranch in this fun cow-patterned romper. An added bonus: it's made entirely with single crochet!

SIZES

Romper: 6–12M (18–24M, 2T, 3T, 4T)

Finished Chest Measurement: 20 (22, 24, 26, 28)"

MATERIALS

A 3 (4, 4, 5, 6) balls Plymouth Wildflower DK (50g, 137yds/ball; 51% cotton, 49% acrylic), Cream 40

B 1 (1, 1, 2, 2) balls Plymouth Wildflower DK, Black 41

C 1 ball Plymouth Wildflower DK, Bright Red 46

Size 5.5 mm (I/9 US) crochet hook or size needed to obtain gauge

4 small snaps or 4 (½"-square) pieces of Velcro

GAUGE

16 sts and 20 rows = 4" in sc

Note: To make cow patt, follow the corresponding charts on pages 28–30.

ROMPER

FRONT AND BACK
Make pant legs: With color A, ch 21 (22, 24, 26, 28).

Row 1: Working color chart at same time, work 1 sc in second ch from hook and in each ch across, ch 1, turn—20 (21, 23, 25, 27) sc.

Row 2: Work 1 sc in each sc across, ch 1, turn.

Rep row 2 until pant leg measures 2½ (2½, 3, 3½, 3½)" from beg. Finish off. Set pant leg aside and rep for other pant leg. When you have finished second pant leg, do not finish off; work as follows:

Next row: Work 1 sc in each sc across. Do not turn your work. Pick up first pant leg and work across last row, cont in patt; this joins the pant legs—40 (42, 46, 50, 54) sc. Ch 1, turn. Beg body.

Rep row 2 until front measures 16½ (17½, 18½, 19½, 20½)" from beg. Finish off.

Rep to make back.

SLEEVES (Make 2)
With color A, ch 33 (35, 37, 39, 41).

Row 1: Work 1 sc in second ch from hook and in each ch across, ch 1, turn—32 (34, 36, 38, 40) sc.

Row 2: Work 1 sc in each sc across, ch 1, turn.

Rep row 2 until sleeve measures 1½ (2, 2½, 2½, 3)" from beg. Finish off.

ASSEMBLY
Join shoulders: With RS of front and back together, stitch 2½ (2¾, 3, 3½, 4)" from outside edge on each shoulder. Attach sleeves: Measure down 4 (4¼, 4½, 4¾, 5)" from shoulder seam on front and back and place markers. Sew in sleeves between markers. Sew side and underarm seams.

FINISHING
Leg Placket (romper back only)
Attach color A to bottom inside of back pant leg.

Row 1: Evenly sc 1 row across inside of both pant legs, ch 1, turn.

Rows 2 and 3: Work 1 sc in each sc across, ch 1, turn.

Row 4: Work 1 sc in each sc across. Finish off.

Attach snaps or Velcro to inside-front and outside-back leg placket.

Trim
With color C, work 1 row sc evenly around neck edge. Finish off.

With color C, work 2 rows sc evenly around sleeves and legs. Finish off.

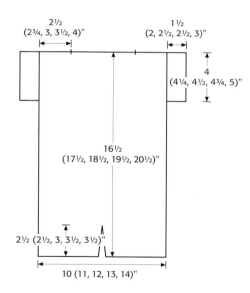

Back

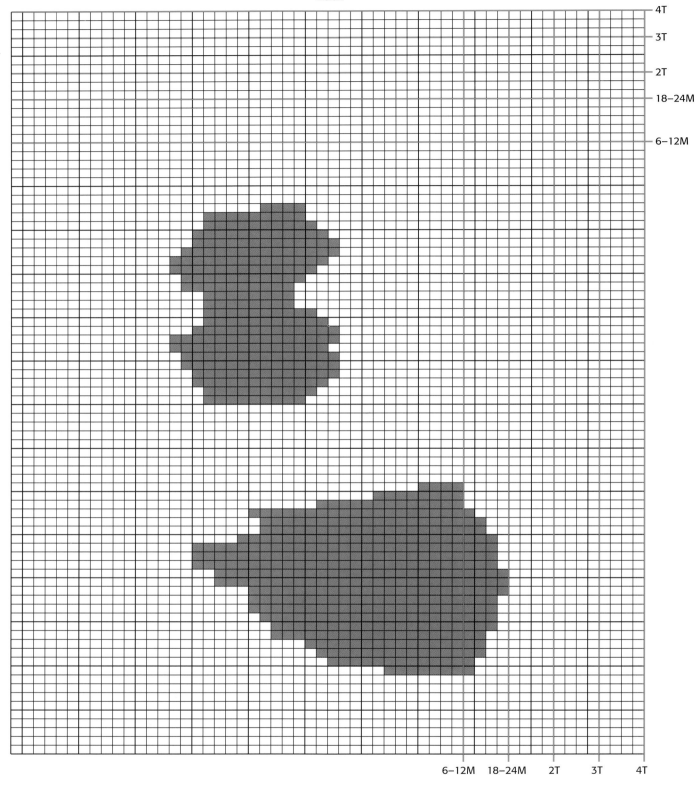

For all cowpoke graphs:

1 square = 1 stitch
1 square = 1 row
4 stitches = 1 inch
5 rows = 1 inch

While working stitch pattern noted above, work color chart at the same time. Read charts upwards from the right hand corner. Follow odd numbered rows from right to left, even numbered rows from left to right. If you miss a square, that's okay. After all, no two cows are alike!

Front

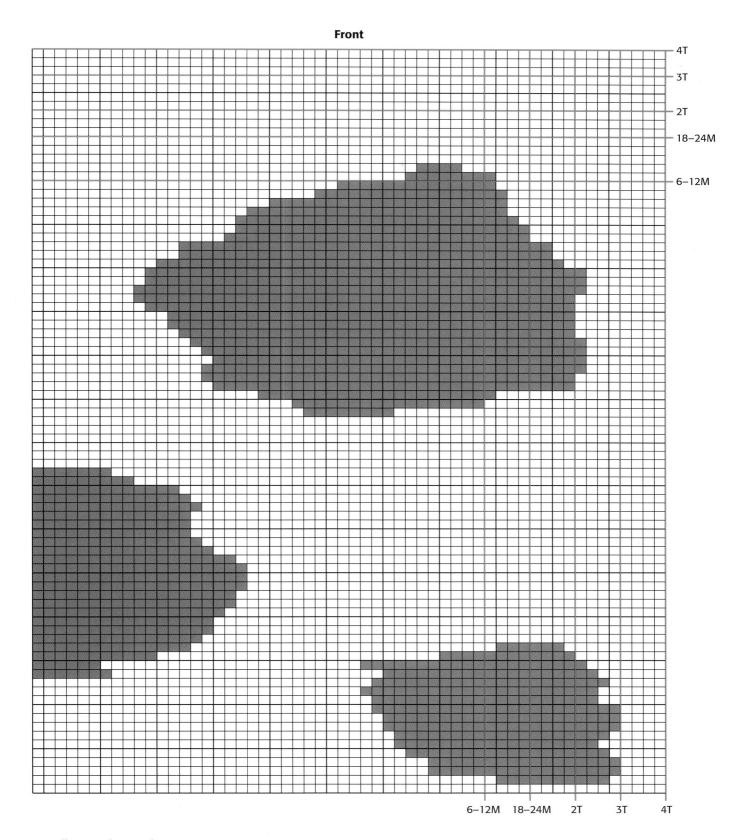

For all cowpoke graphs:
1 square = 1 stitch
1 square = 1 row
4 stitches = 1 inch
5 rows = 1 inch

Left Sleeve

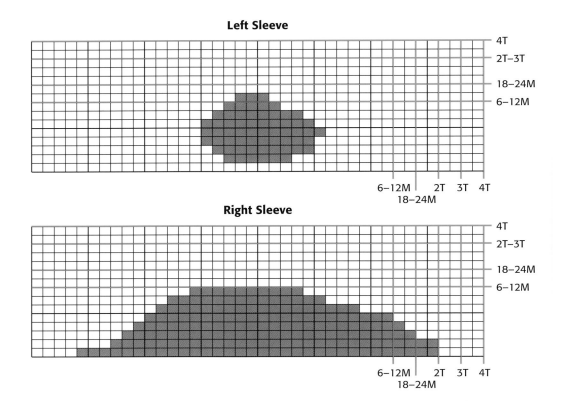

4T
2T–3T
18–24M
6–12M

6–12M   2T   3T   4T
18–24M

Right Sleeve

4T
2T–3T
18–24M
6–12M

6–12M   2T   3T   4T
18–24M

Left Front Leg

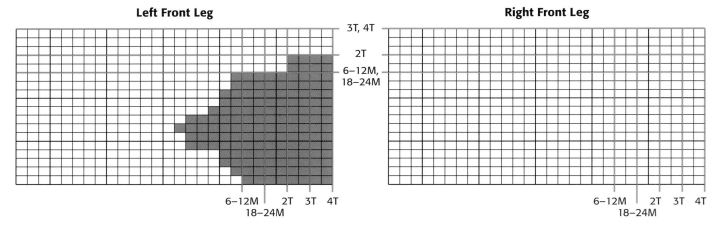

3T, 4T
2T
6–12M,
18–24M

6–12M   2T   3T   4T
18–24M

Right Front Leg

6–12M   2T   3T   4T
18–24M

Left Back Leg

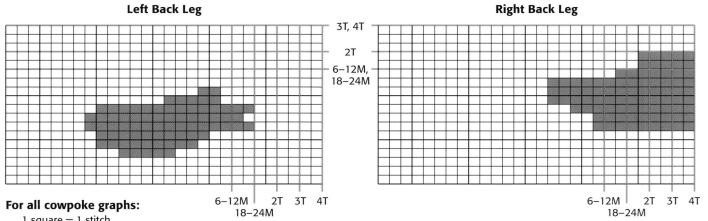

3T, 4T
2T
6–12M,
18–24M

6–12M   2T   3T   4T
18–24M

Right Back Leg

6–12M   2T   3T   4T
18–24M

For all cowpoke graphs:
1 square = 1 stitch
1 square = 1 row
4 stitches = 1 inch
5 rows = 1 inch

COCO CARDIGAN
AND CHAPEAU

Inspired by Coco Chanel, our cardigan has updated three-quarter-length sleeves, popcorn buttons, and white trim on a cotton-candy-pink background. The look would not be complete without a matching chapeau.

SIZES

Cardigan: 6–12M (18M, 24M, 2T, 3T, 4T)

Finished Chest Measurement: 20 (22, 24, 26, 28, 30)"

Chapeau: Small (Medium, Large)

Circumference: 17 (19, 21)"

MATERIALS

A 4 (4, 5, 6, 7, 8) balls Plymouth Wildflower DK (50g, 137yds/ball; 51% cotton, 49% acrylic), Cotton Candy Pink 54

B 1 ball Plymouth Wildflower DK, White 41

Size 5.5 mm (I/9 US) crochet hook or size needed to obtain gauge

GAUGE

16 sts and 20 rows = 4" in sc

CARDIGAN

BACK

With color A, ch 41 (45, 49, 53, 57, 61).

Row 1: Work 1 sc in second ch from hook and in each ch across, ch 1, turn—40 (44, 48, 52, 56, 60) sc.

Row 2: Work 1 sc in each sc across, ch 1, turn. Rep row 2 until back measures 9½ (10½, 11½, 12½, 13½, 14½)" from beg. Finish off.

FRONT (Make 2)

With color A, ch 21 (23, 25, 27, 29, 31).

Row 1: Work 1 sc in second ch from hook and in each ch across, ch 1, turn—20 (22, 24, 26, 28, 30) sc.

Row 2: Work 1 sc in each sc across, ch 1, turn. Rep row 2 until front measures 7½ (8½, 9½, 10½, 11½, 12½)" from beg. Beg neck shaping.

NECK SHAPING

Next row: Work 1 sc in next 15 (17, 19, 20, 22, 24) sc, sk rem sc, ch 1, turn.

Next 4 (4, 4, 5, 5, 5) rows: Dec 1 st at neck edge and sc across row—11 (13, 15, 15, 17, 19) sc.

Rep row 2 until front measures 9½ (10½, 11½, 12½, 13½, 14½)" from beg. Finish off.

SLEEVES (Make 2)

With color A, ch 25 (27, 29, 31, 33, 35).

Row 1: Work 1 sc in second ch from hook and in each ch across, ch 1, turn—24 (26, 28, 30, 32, 34) sc.

Rows 2, 3, and 4: Work 1 sc in each sc across, ch 1, turn.

Row 5: Work 2 sc in first sc, 1 sc in each sc across until 1 sc remains, 2 sc in last sc in row, ch 1, turn—26 (28, 30, 32, 34, 36) sc.

Rep rows 1–5 until sleeve measures 5 (5½, 6, 6½, 7, 7½)" from beg—34 (36, 40, 42, 46, 48) sc. Finish off.

ASSEMBLY

Join shoulders: With RS of front and back together, sew 2¾ (3¼, 3½, 3¾, 4½, 4½)" from outside edge on each shoulder. Attach sleeves: Measure down 4¼ (4½, 5, 5¼, 5¾, 6)" from shoulder seam on front and back and place markers. Sew in sleeves between markers. Sew side and underarm seams.

FINISHING

With color A, sc 2 rows evenly around neck edge.

FRONT PLACKET (Buttonhole Side)

Row 1: With RS facing, attach color A at lower left front edge and work 30 (34, 38, 42, 46, 50) sc evenly spaced along front, ch 1, turn.

Row 2: Work 1 sc in 1 (1, 2, 2, 2, 2) sc, sk next sc, ch 1, *work 1 sc in next 8 (9, 10, 8, 9, 10) sc, sk next sc, ch 1*; rep from * to * another 2 (2, 2, 3, 3, 3) times, work 1 sc in each of last 1 (2, 2, 3, 3, 3) sc, ch 1, turn.

Row 3: Work 1 sc in each sc or ch across.

Row 4: Work 1 sc in each sc across. Finish off.

FRONT PLACKET (Button Side)

Row 1: With RS facing, attach color A at edge and work 30 (34, 38, 42, 46, 50) sc evenly spaced along front edge, ch 1, turn.

Rows 2 and 3: Work 1 sc in each sc across, ch 1, turn.

Row 4: Work 1 sc in each sc across. Finish off.

Popcorn Buttons

Use buttonholes as spacing guides and attach 4 (4, 4, 5, 5, 5) buttons. With color B, attach yarn around fp with a sl st, and in the same fp, work 1 sc, 4 dc, 1 sc. Then insert hook into first sc of button, yo, and finish off.

Trim

With color B, work 1 row of sc around neck, front placket, bottom edge, and sleeve cuff. Ease yarn around corners by working 3 sc in each corner. Finish off.

CHAPEAU

TOP

Small: Complete rnds 1–12 only.

Medium: Complete rnds 1–14 only.

Large: Complete all rnds.

Note: Mark beg of rnds. Work rnds continuously; do not join.

With color A, ch 2.

Rnd 1: Work 6 sc in second ch from hook.

Rnd 2: Work 2 sc in each sc around—12 sc.

Rnd 3: *Work 1 sc in next sc, 2 sc in next sc*; rep from * to * 6 times—18 sc.

Rnd 4: *Work 1 sc in next sc, 2 sc in next sc*; rep from * to * 9 times—27 sc.

Rnd 5: *Work 1 sc in next 2 sc, 2 sc in next sc*; rep from * to * 9 times—36 sc.

Rnds 6, 8, 10, 12, and 14: Work 1 sc in each sc around.

Rnd 7: *Work 1 sc in next 3 sc, 2 sc in next sc*; rep from * to * 9 times—45 sc.

Rnd 9: *Work 1 sc in next 4 sc, 2 sc in next sc*; rep from * to * 9 times—54 sc.

Rnd 11: *Work 1 sc in next 5 sc, 2 sc in next sc*; rep from * to * 9 times—63 sc.

Rnd 13: *Work 1 sc in next 6 sc, 2 sc in next sc*; rep from * to * 9 times—72 sc.

Rnd 15: *Work 1 sc in next 7 sc, 2 sc in next sc*; rep from * to * 9 times—81 sc.

Rnd 16: Work 1 sc in each sc around. Finish off.

SIDES

With color A, ch 64 (73, 82).

Row 1: Work 1 sc in second ch from hook and in each ch across, ch 1, turn—63 (72, 81) sc.

Row 2: Work 1 sc in each sc across, ch 1, turn.

Rep row 2 another 8 (10, 12) times. Switch to color B and work another 2 rows. Finish off.

ASSEMBLY

With RS of side panels together, sew ends together. Turn panel RS out and join to top with sc around outside edge. Add brim.

BRIM

Small: Complete rnds 1–6.

Medium: Complete rnds 1, 2, and 5–8.

Large: Complete rnds 1, 2, and 7–10.

Rnd 1: At hat bottom, attach color A and sc in each sc around—63 (72, 81) sc.

Rounds 2, 4, 6, and 8: Work 1 sc in each sc around.

Rnd 3: *Work 1 sc in next 6 sc, 2 sc in next sc*; rep from * to * 9 times—72 sc.

Rnd 5: *Work 1 sc in next 7 sc, 2 sc in next sc*; rep from * to * 9 times—81 sc.

Rnd 7: *Work 1 sc in next 8 sc, 2 sc in next sc*; rep from * to * 9 times—90 sc.

Rnd 9: *Work 1 sc in next 9 sc, 2 sc in next sc*; rep from * to * 9 times—99 sc.

Rnd 10: Work 1 sc in each sc around. Finish off.

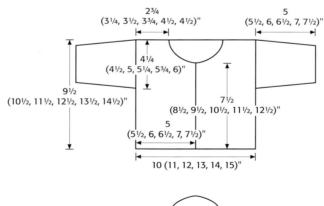

Chapeau

17 (19, 21)"

Peppermint Twist Pullover and Pants

Cotton-candy pink, lime green, and soft pink were mixed together to make the Peppermint Twist set. Full sleeves, scalloped edges, contrasting waistband, and a relaxed fit are a few of the details on this whimsical pullover and coordinating pants.

SIZES

Pullover: 6–12M (18–24M, 2T–3T, 4T)

Finished Chest Measurement: 18 (24, 24, 30)"

Pants: 6–12M (18–24M, 2T–3T, 4T)

Finished Waist Measurement: 16 (17, 18, 19)"

MATERIALS

A 3 (4, 5, 6) balls Plymouth Wildflower DK (50g, 137yds/ball; 51% cotton, 49% acrylic), Lime 58

B 1 (1, 1, 2) balls Plymouth Wildflower DK, Light Pink 53

C 2 (2, 3, 3) balls Plymouth Wildflower DK, Cotton Candy Pink 54

Size 5.5 mm (I/9 US) crochet hook or size needed to obtain gauge

1 yd. of ¾"-wide elastic band

GAUGE

16 sts and 20 rows = 4" in sc

PULLOVER

FRONT AND BACK

With color A, ch 39 (48, 48, 57).

Row 1: Work 1 sc in second ch from hook, 1 sc in next ch, *1 hdc in next 2 ch, 1 dc in next 3 ch, 1 hdc in next 2 ch, 1 sc in next 2 ch*; rep from * to * across, ch 1, turn—38 (47, 47, 56) sts.

Row 2: Work 1 sc in first 2 sc, *1 hdc in next 2 hdc, 1 dc in next 3 dc, 1 hdc in next 2 hdc, 1 sc in next 2 sc*; rep from * to * across. Change to color B, ch 1, turn.

Row 3: Work 1 sc in each st across. Change to color C, ch 3 (counts as first dc on following rows), turn.

Row 4: Sk first sc, work 1 dc in next sc, *1 hdc in next 2 sc, 1 sc in next 3 sc, 1 hdc in next 2 sc, 1 dc in next 2 sc*; rep from * to * across, ch 3, turn.

Row 5: Sk first dc, work 1 dc in next dc, *1 hdc in next 2 hdc, 1 sc in next 3 sc, 1 hdc in next 2 hdc, 1 dc in next 2 dc*; rep from * to * across. Change to color B, ch 1, turn.

Row 6: Work 1 sc in each st across. Change to color A, ch 1, turn.

Row 7: Work 1 sc in first 2 sc, *1 hdc in next 2 sc, 1 dc in next 3 sc, 1 hdc in next 2 sc, 1 sc in next 2 sc*; rep from * to * across, ch 1, turn.

Row 8: Work 1 sc in first 2 sc, *1 hdc in next 2 hdc, 1 dc in next 3 dc, 1 hdc in next 2 hdc, 1 sc in next 2 sc*; rep from * to * across. Change to color B, ch 1, turn.

Rep rows 3–8 another 4 (5, 6, 7) times.

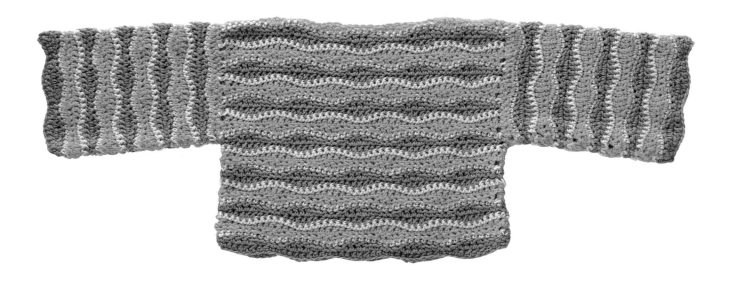

Next row: Work 1 sc in each st across. Change to color C, ch 3, turn.

Last row: Sk first sc, work 1 dc in next sc, *1 hdc in next 2 sc, 1 sc in next 3 sc, 1 hdc in next 2 sc, 1 dc in next 2 sc*; rep from * to * across. Finish off. Rep to make back.

SLEEVES (Make 2)
With color A, ch 39 (39, 48, 48).

Row 1: Work 1 sc in second ch from hook, 1 sc in next ch, *1 hdc in next 2 ch, 1 dc in next 3 ch, 1 hdc in next 2 ch, 1 sc in next 2 ch*; rep from * to * across, ch 1, turn—38 (38, 47, 47) sts.

Row 2: Work 1 sc in first 2 sc, *1 hdc in next 2 hdc, 1 dc in next 3 dc, 1 hdc in next 2 hdc, 1 sc in next 2 sc*; rep from * to * across. Change to color B, ch 1, turn.

Row 3: Work 1 sc in each st across. Change to color C, ch 3, turn.

Row 4: Sk first sc, work 1 dc in next sc, *1 hdc in next 2 sc, 1 sc in next 3 sc, 1 hdc in next 2 sc, 1 dc in next 2 sc*; rep from * to * across, ch 3, turn.

Row 5: Sk first dc, work 1 dc in next dc, *1 hdc in next 2 hdc, 1 sc in next 3 sc, 1 hdc in next 2 hdc, 1 dc in next 2 dc*; rep from * to * across. Change to color B, ch 1, turn.

Row 6: Work 1 sc in each st across. Change to color A, ch 1, turn.

Row 7: Work 1 sc in first 2 sc, *1 hdc in next 2 sc, 1 dc in next 3 sc, 1 hdc in next 2 sc, 1 sc in next 2 sc*; rep from * to * across, ch 1, turn.

Row 8: Work 1 sc in first 2 sc, *1 hdc in next 2 hdc, 1 dc in next 3 dc, 1 hdc in next 2 hdc, 1 sc in next 2 sc*; rep from * to * across. Change to color B, ch 1, turn.

Rep rows 3–8 another 2 (3, 3, 4) times.

Next row: Work 1 sc in each st across. Change to color C, ch 3, turn.

Last row: Sk first sc, work 1 dc in next sc, *1 hdc in next 2 sc, 1 sc in next 3 sc, 1 hdc in next 2 sc, 1 dc in next 2 sc*; rep from * to * across. Finish off.

ASSEMBLY
Join shoulders: With RS of front and back together, sew 3 (3½, 4, 4½)" from outside edge on each shoulder. Attach sleeves: Measure down 4½ (4½, 6, 6)" from shoulder seam on front and back and place markers. Sew in sleeves between markers. Sew side and under-arm seams.

PANTS
The pants are worked from the bottom up.

SIDE PANELS (Make 2)
With color A, ch 48 (48, 57, 57).

Row 1: Work 1 sc in second ch from hook, 1 sc in next ch, *1 hdc in next 2 ch, 1 dc in next 3 ch, 1 hdc in next 2 ch, 1 sc in next 2 ch*; rep from * to * across, ch 1, turn—47 (47, 56, 56) sts.

Row 2: Work 1 sc in first 2 sc, *1 hdc in next 2 hdc, 1 dc in next 3 dc, 1 hdc in next 2 hdc, 1 sc in next 2 sc*; rep from * to * across. Change to color B, ch 1, turn.

Row 3: Work 1 sc in each st across. Change to color C, ch 3, turn.

Row 4: Sk first sc, work 1 dc in next sc, *1 hdc in next 2 sc, 1 sc in next 3 sc, 1 hdc in next 2 sc, 1 dc in next 2 sc*; rep from * to * across, ch 3, turn.

Row 5: Sk first dc, work 1 dc in next dc, *1 hdc in next 2 hdc, 1 sc in next 3 sc, 1 hdc in next 2 hdc, 1 dc in next 2 dc*; rep from * to * across. Change to color B, ch 1, turn.

Row 6: Work 1 sc in each st across. Change to color A, ch 1, turn.

Row 7: Work 1 sc in first 2 sc, *1 hdc in next 2 sc, 1 dc in next 3 sc, 1 hdc in next 2 sc, 1 sc in next 2 sc*; rep from * to * across, ch 1, turn.

Row 8: Sk first sc, work 1 hdc in next sc and in each st across, ch 2, turn—47 (47, 56, 56) sts.

Row 9: Sk first hdc, work 1 hdc in next hdc and in each hdc across, ch 2, turn.

Rep row 9 until side panel measures 5 (5½, 6½, 7½)" from beg. Do not finish off. Beg crotch shaping.

CROTCH SHAPING

Dec 2 hdc at end of next 4 rows as follows: Sk first hdc, work 1 hdc in next hdc and in each hdc across to last 3 sts, dec 2 hdc, ch 2, turn. (Need help decreasing? See page 16.)

Rep row 9 until side panel measures 12½ (13½, 14, 15)" from beg. Finish off.

ASSEMBLY

With RS facing, sew front and back center seams and then inside leg seams.

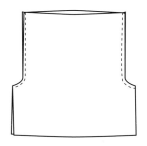

Sew front to back.

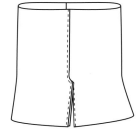

Sew inside leg seams.

FINISHING

Waistband

With color C, attach yarn to top of pants.

Rnd 1: Work 1 hdc in each hdc around, join in first hdc, ch 2.

Rnd 2: Work 1 hdc in each hdc around, join in second ch of beg ch-2 sp, ch 2.

Rep rnd 2 another 6 times. Finish off.

To make casing, fold waistband down around outside edge. Sew seam, leaving an opening to insert elastic. Cut elastic 16½ (17½, 18½, 19½)". Insert elastic through casing. Lap ends ½" and stitch together. Sew opening in casing closed.

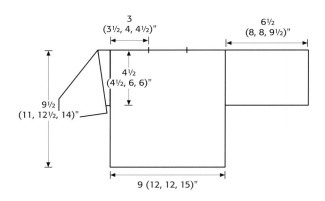

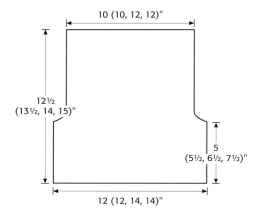

Sweet Pea Pullover and Chapeau

Soft colors of sun-kissed yellow and celadon green combine to make this delicate set. The oversized chapeau and cropped sweater with three-quarter-length sleeves are trimmed with ruffles and bubbles to mimic leaves and peas plucked right from the garden.

SIZES

Pullover: 6–12M (18–24M, 2T–3T, 4T)

Finished Chest Measurement: 21 (24, 27, 30)"

Chapeau: Small (Medium, Large)

Circumference: 17 (19, 21)"

MATERIALS

A 4 (5, 6, 7) balls Plymouth Wildflower DK (50g, 137yds/ball; 51% cotton, 49% acrylic), Yellow 41

B 1 (1, 2, 2) balls Plymouth Wildflower DK, Celadon Green 19

Size 5.5 mm (I/9 US) crochet hook or size needed to obtain gauge

GAUGE

16 sts and 20 rows = 4" in sc

SWEATER

Bubble stitch: Yo, insert hook into next st, *yo, draw lp through, yo, draw through 2 lps*; rep from * to * another 4 times, yo, draw through 6 lps.

BACK

With color A, ch 43 (49, 55, 61).

Row 1: Work 1 sc in second ch from hook and in each ch across, ch 1, turn—42 (48, 54, 60) sc.

Rows 2 and 3: Work 1 sc in each sc across, ch 1, turn.

Row 4: Change to color B; rep row 2.

Row 5: *Work 1 bubble st in next sc, sc in next 2 sc*; rep from * to * to end, ch 1, turn.

Row 6: Change to color A, work 1 sc in each sc and 1 sc in top of each bubble st across.

Rep row 2 until back measures 10½ (12, 13½, 15)" from beg. Finish off.

FRONT

Work as for back until front measures 8¾ (10, 11½, 12½)" from beg. Beg neck shaping.

NECK SHAPING

Row 1: Work 1 sc in first 16 (19, 21, 24) sc, sk next 10 (10, 12, 12) sc; with a second ball of yarn, work 1 sc in rem 16 (19, 21, 24) sc.

Next 4 (4, 5, 5) rows: Work across each row, dec 1 sc at neck edge—12 (15, 16, 19) sts rem on each side.

All rem rows: Work 1 sc in each sc across, ch 1, turn. Rep until front measures 10½ (12, 13½, 15)" from beg. Finish off.

SLEEVES (Make 2)

With color A, ch 46 (46, 49, 49).

Row 1: Work 1 sc in second ch from hook and each ch across, ch 1, turn—45 (45, 48, 48) sc.

Row 2: Work 1 sc in each sc across, ch 1, turn.

Rep row 2 until sleeve measures 5 (5½, 6, 6½)" from beg.

TRIM

Row 1: Change to color B, work 1 sc in each sc across.

Row 2: *Work 1 bubble st in next sc, sc in next 2 sc*; rep from * to * across, ch 1, turn.

Row 3: Change to color A, work 1 sc in each sc and 1 sc in top of each bubble.

Row 4 (sizes 6–12M and 18–24M): *Work 1 sc in next sc, dec 1 sc over next 2 sc*; rep from * to * across, ch 1, turn—30 sc.

Row 4 (sizes 2T–3T, and 4T): *Sc in next 2 sc, dec 1 sc over next 2 sc*; rep from * to * across, ch 1, turn—36 sc.

Row 5: Change to color B, work 1 sc in each sc across.

Row 6: *Work 1 sc in first sc, sk next sc, work 2 dc in next sc, ch 1, work 2 dc in next sc, sk next sc, work 1 sc in next sc*; rep from * to * across, ch 1, turn.

Row 7: *Work 1 sc in first sc, ch 2, sk next 2 dc, work 7 dc in next ch-1 sp, ch 2, sk next 2 dc, work 1 sc in next sc*; rep from * to * across. Finish off.

ASSEMBLY

Join shoulders: With RS of front and back together, sew 3 (3¾, 4, 4¾)" from outside edge on each shoulder. Attach sleeves: Measure down 5½ (5½, 6, 6)" from shoulder seam on front and back and place markers. Sew in sleeves between markers. Sew side and underarm seams.

FINISHING
Collar
Rnd 1: With color B, work 48 (48, 54, 54) sc evenly around neck edge. Join with sl st to first sc in row, ch 1, turn.

Rnd 2: *Work 1 sc in first sc, sk next sc, work 2 dc in next sc, ch 1, work 2 dc in next sc, sk next sc, work 1 sc in next sc*; rep from * to * around, ch 1, turn.

Rnd 3: *Work 1 sc in first sc, ch 2, sk next 2 dc, work 7 dc in next ch-1 sp, ch 2, sk next 2 dc, work 1 sc in next sc*; rep from * to * around. Finish off.

CHAPEAU

Small: Complete rnds 1–18, 27–33, and 35–44.

Medium: Complete all rnds except rnds 34 and 37.

Large: Complete all rnds except rnds 35–37.

Rnd 1: With color A, ch 2, work 6 sc in second ch from hook.

Rnd 2: Work 1 sc in first sc, then 2 sc in each sc around, join with sl st to first sc, ch 1—11 sc.

Rnd 3: Work 2 sc in each sc; rep 11 times; join with sl st to first sc, ch 1—22 sc.

Rnds 4, 6, 8, 10, 12, 14, 16, and 18: Work 1 sc in each sc, join with sl st to first sc, ch 1.

Rnd 5: *Work 1 sc in next sc, 2 sc in next sc*; rep from * to * 11 times, join with sl st to first sc, ch 1—33 sc.

Rnd 7: *Work 1 sc in next 2 sc, 2 sc in next sc*; rep from * to * 11 times, join with sl st to first sc, ch 1—44 sc.

Rnd 9: *Work 1 sc in next 3 sc, 2 sc in next sc*; rep from * to * 11 times, join with sl st to first sc, ch 1—55 sc.

Rnd 11: *Work 1 sc in next 4 sc, 2 sc in next sc*; rep from * to * 11 times, join with sl st to first sc, ch 1—66 sc.

Rnd 13: *Work 1 sc in next 5 sc, 2 sc in next sc*; rep from * to * 11 times, join with sl st to first sc, ch 1—77 sc.

Rnd 15: *Work 1 sc in next 6 sc, 2 sc in next sc*; rep from * to * 11 times, join with sl st to first sc, ch 1—88 sc.

Rnd 17: *Work 1 sc in next 7 sc, 2 sc in next sc*; rep from * to * 11 times, join with sl st to first sc, ch 1—99 sc.

Rnd 19: *Work 1 sc in next 8 sc, 2 sc in next sc*; rep from * to * 11 times, join with sl st to first sc, ch 1—110 sc.

Rnds 20–25: Work 1 sc in each sc around, join with sl st to first sc, ch 1.

Rnd 26: *Work 1 sc in next 8 sc, dec 1 sc over next 2 sc*; rep from * to * 11 times, join with sl st to first sc, ch 1—99 sc.

Rnds 27–32: Work 1 sc in each sc around, join with sl st to first sc, ch 1.

Rnd 33: *Work 1 sc in next 9 sc, dec 1 sc over next 2 sc*; rep from * to * 9 times, join with sl st to first sc, ch 1—90 sc.

Rnd 34: *Work 1 sc in next 13 sc, dec 1 sc over next 2 sc*; rep from * to * 6 times, join with sl st to first sc, ch 1—84 sc.

Rnd 35: *Work 1 sc in next 8 sc, dec 1 sc over next 2 sc*; rep from * to * 9 times, join with sl st to first sc, ch 1—81 sc.

Rnd 36: *Work 1 sc in next 7 sc, dec 1 sc over next 2 sc*; rep from * to * 9 times, join with sl st to first sc, ch 1—72 sc.

Rnd 37: *Work 1 sc in next 4 sc, dec 1 sc over next 2 sc*; rep from * to * 12 times, join with sl st to first sc, ch 1—60 sc.

Rnd 38: Change to color B, *work 1 bubble st in next sc, 1 sc in next 2 sc*; rep from * to *, join with sl st to first sc, ch 1.

Rnd 39: Work 1 sc in each sc around, join with sl st to first sc, ch 1.

Rnd 40: Change to color A, work 1 sc in each sc around, join with sl st to first sc, ch 1.

Rnd 41: Work 1 sc in each sc around, join with sl st to first sc, ch 1.

Rnd 42: Change to color B, work 1 sc in each sc around, join with sl st to first sc, ch 1.

Rnd 43: *Work 1 sc in first sc, sk next sc, work 2 dc in next sc, ch 1, work 2 dc in next sc, sk next sc, work 1 sc in next sc*; rep from * to *, join with sl st to first sc, ch 1.

Rnd 44: *Work 1 sc in first sc, ch 2, sk next 2 dc, work 7 dc in next ch-1 sp, ch 2, sk next 2 dc, work 1 sc in next sc*; rep from * to *, join with sl st to first sc. Finish off.

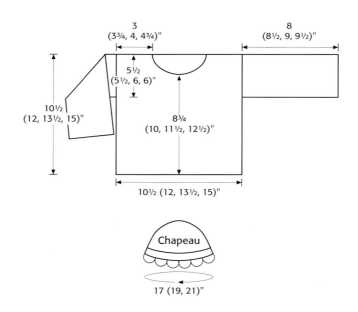

QUACK-AND-WADDLE ROMPER WITH FINGER PUPPET

Go wading in your favorite pond in this fun and fresh romper. It's crocheted in a relaxed textured stitch, making it cool and comfortable. The fun never ends with the special pocket made just for a ducky finger puppet!

SIZES

Romper: 6–12M (18–24M, 2T, 3T, 4T)

Finished Chest Measurement: 20 (22, 24, 26, 28)"

MATERIALS

A 4 (4, 5, 5, 6) balls Plymouth Wildflower DK (50g, 137yds/ball; 51% cotton, 49% acrylic), Light Blue 70

B 1 ball Plymouth Wildflower DK, Tangerine 56

C 1 ball Plymouth Wildflower DK, Yellow 48

12" length of black embroidery floss

Size 5.5 mm (I/9 US) crochet hook or size needed to obtain gauge (for romper)

Size 3.75 mm (F/5 US) crochet hook (for finger puppet)

4 small snaps or 4 (½"-square) pieces of Velcro

GAUGE

16 sts and 20 rows = 4" in sc

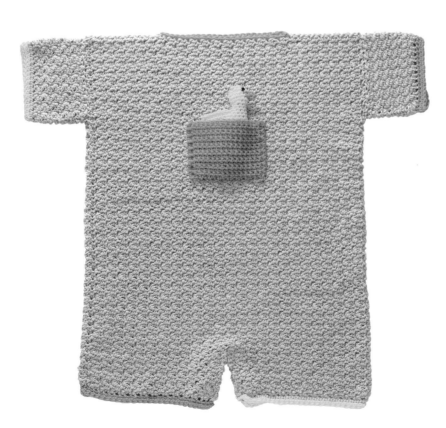

ROMPER

FRONT AND BACK

Pant Legs: With color A, ch 19 (21, 23, 25, 27).

Row 1: Work 1 sc in second ch from hook, 1 dc in next ch, *1 sc in next ch, 1 dc in next ch*; rep from * to * across, ch 1, turn—18 (20, 22, 24, 26) sts.

Row 2: Work 1 sc in first dc, 1 dc in next sc, *1 sc in next dc, 1 dc in next sc*; rep from * to * across, ch 1, turn.

Rep row 2 until pant leg measures 2 (2, 2, 2½, 2½)" from beg. Finish off. Set pant leg aside and rep for other pant leg, but do not finish off.

Next row: Work 1 sc in first dc, 1 dc in next sc, *1 sc in next dc, 1 dc in next sc*; rep from * to * across. Do not turn work. Pick up first pant leg and work across last row, cont patt; this will join the pant legs—36 (40, 44, 48, 52) sts across. Ch 1, turn.

Rep row 2 until front measures 16½ (17, 17½, 18½, 19½)" from beg. Finish off. Rep to make back.

SLEEVES (Make 2)

With color A, ch 31 (31, 35, 35, 37).

Row 1: Work 1 sc in second ch from hook, 1 dc in next ch, *1 sc in next ch, 1dc in next ch*; rep from * to * across, ch 1, turn—30 (30, 34, 34, 36) sts.

Row 2: Work 1 sc in first dc, 1 dc in next sc, *1 sc in next dc, 1 dc in next sc*; rep from * to * across, ch 1, turn.

Rep row 2 until sleeve measures 1½ (2, 2½, 2½, 3)" from beg. Finish off.

POCKET

With color B, ch 17.

Row 1: Work 1 sc in second ch from hook and in each ch across—16 sc.

Row 2: Work 1 sc in each sc across.

Rep row 2 until pocket measures 3½" from beg. Finish off.

ASSEMBLY

Join shoulders: With RS of front and back together, sew 2½ (2¾, 3, 3½, 4)" from outside edge on each shoulder. Attach sleeves: Measure down 4 (4, 4½, 4½, 5)" from shoulder seam on front and back and place markers. Sew in sleeves between markers. Sew side and underarm seams.

FINISHING

Attach pocket to romper: Measure down 3½ (3½, 4½, 4½, 5)" from neck edge and place top edge of pocket. Center pocket, and with color B, stitch sides and bottom, making sure to sew through both pocket and romper. Finish off.

Leg Placket (on romper back only)

Attach color A to bottom of inside-back pant leg.

Row 1: Evenly sc 1 row across inside of both pant legs, ch 1, turn.

Next 3 rows: Work 1 sc in each sc across, ch 1, turn. Finish off.

Attach snaps or Velcro to inside-front and outside-back leg placket.

Trim

With color B, work 1 row sc evenly around neck edge. Finish off.

With color B, work 2 rows sc evenly around right sleeve and left leg. Finish off.

With color C, work 2 rows sc evenly around left sleeve and right leg. Finish off.

FINGER PUPPET

Note: Mark beg of rnds. Rnds are worked continuously; do not join.

With smallest crochet hook and color B, ch 12. Join with sl st to first ch.

Rnd 1: Work 1 sc in each ch around—12 sc.

Rnds 2–5: Work 1 sc in each sc around.

Rnd 6: Work 1 sc in each sc around. At end of row, change to color C.

Rnd 7: Work 2 sc in each sc around—24 sc.

Rnds 8–15: Work 1 sc in each sc around.

Rnd 16: Shape neck by working 1 sc in first 4 sc, sk next 16 sc (you will no longer work these 16 sts), sc in last 4 sc.

Rnd 17: Work 1 sc in each sc around—8 sc.

Rnd 18: *Work 1 sc in next sc, 2 sc in next sc*; rep from * to * around—12 sc.

Rnds 19 and 20: Work 1 sc in each sc around.

Rnd 21: *Work 1 sc in next sc, dec 1 sc over next 2 sc*; rep from * to * around—8 sc.

Rnd 22: *Dec 1 sc over next 2 sc*; rep from * to * around—4 sc.

Rnd 23: *Dec 1 sc over next 2 sc*; rep from * to * around—2 sc. Finish off.

Attach color C to back at base of neck and sc across row to join sides together. Finish off.

BEAK

Attach color B to head front, 2 rows down from top.

Row 1: Work 2 sc in fp, ch 1, turn.

Row 2: Work 2 sc in each sc, ch 1, turn.

Row 3: Dec 1 sc. Finish off.

EYES

With embroidery floss, stitch eyes just above beak.

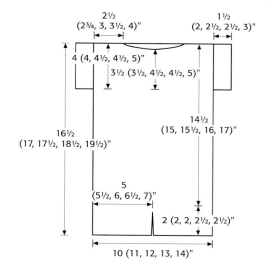

Lady-in-Waiting Cardigan

This quick-to-make cardigan will be a favorite for your little lady. The celadon green background is accented by soft pink trim on the sleeves, waistband, and bow. Full, three-quarter-length sleeves and a turned collar finish the look.

SKILL LEVEL: ADVANCED BEGINNER

SIZES

Cardigan: 6–12M (18M, 24M, 2T, 3T, 4T)

Finished Chest Measurement: 20 (22, 24, 26, 28, 30)"

MATERIALS

A 4 (5, 5, 6, 7, 7) balls Plymouth Wildflower DK (50g, 137yds/ball; 51% cotton, 49% acrylic), Celadon Green 19

B 1 (1, 1, 2, 2, 2) balls Plymouth Wildflower DK, Light Pink 53

Size 5.5 mm (I/9 US) crochet hook or size needed to obtain gauge

GAUGE

16 sts and 20 rows = 4" in sc

CARDIGAN

The back and fronts are worked from the top down.

BACK

With color A, ch 38 (42, 46, 50, 54, 58).

Row 1: Work 1 sc in second ch from hook and in each ch across, ch 1, turn—37 (41, 45, 49, 53, 57) sc.

Row 2: Work 1 sc in first sc, *sk next sc, work 3 dc in next sc, sk next sc, work 1 sc in next sc*; rep from * to * across to last 4 sts, sk next sc, work 3 dc in next sc, sk next sc, work 1 sc in last sc, ch 3, turn—9 (10, 11, 12, 13, 14) shells made.

Row 3: Work 1 dc in same sc, *sk next dc, work 1 sc in next dc, sk next dc, work 3 dc in next sc*; rep from * to * across to last 4 sts, sk next dc, work 1 sc in next dc, sk next dc, work 2 dc in last sc, ch 1, turn—1 half shell, 8 (9, 10, 11, 12, 13) shells, 1 half shell.

Rep rows 2 and 3 until back measures 9 (10, 11, 11, 12, 13)".

Change to color B, rep rows 2 and 3 for next 2 (2, 2, 4, 4, 4) rows. Back measures 10 (11, 12, 13, 14, 15)" from beg. Finish off.

FRONT (Make 2)
With color A, ch 18 (22, 26, 26, 30, 30).

Row 1: Work 1 sc in second ch from hook and in each ch across, ch 1, turn—17 (21, 25, 25, 29, 29) sc.

Row 2: Work 1 sc in first sc, sk next sc, *work 3 dc in next sc, sk next sc, work 1 sc in next sc, sk next sc*; rep from * to * across to last 3 sts, work 3 dc in next sc, sk next sc, work 1 sc in last sc, ch 3, turn—4 (5, 6, 6, 7, 7) shells made.

Row 3: Work 1 dc in same sc, *sk next dc, work 1 sc in next dc, sk next dc, work 3 dc in next sc*; rep from * to * across to last 4 sts, sk next dc, work 1 sc in next dc, sk next dc, work 2 dc in last sc, ch 1, turn—1 half shell, 3 (4, 5, 5, 6, 6) shells, 1 half shell.

Rep rows 2 and 3 until front measures 9 (10, 11, 11, 12, 13)".

Change to color B, rep rows 2 and 3 for next 2 (2, 2, 4, 4, 4) rows. Front measures 10 (11, 12, 13, 14, 15)" from beg. Finish off.

SLEEVES (Make 2)
With color A, ch 38 (38, 42, 42, 46, 46).

Row 1: Work 1 sc in second ch from hook and in each ch across, ch 1, turn—37 (37, 41, 41, 45, 45) sc.

Row 2: Work 1 sc in first sc, sk next sc, *work 3 dc in next sc, sk next sc, work 1 sc in next sc, sk next sc*; rep from * to * across to last 3 sts, work 3 dc in next sc, sk next sc, work 1 sc in last sc, ch 3, turn—9 (9, 10, 10, 11, 11) shells made.

Row 3: Work 1 dc in same sc, *sk next dc, work 1 sc in next dc, sk next dc, work 3 dc in next sc*; rep from * to * across to last 4 sts, sk next dc, work 1 sc in next dc, sk next dc, work 2 dc in last sc, ch 1, turn—1 half shell, 8 (8, 9, 9, 10, 10) shells, 1 half shell.

Rep rows 2 and 3 until sleeve measures 4½ (5, 5½, 5, 6, 7)".

Change to color B, rep rows 2 and 3 for next 2 (2, 2, 4, 4, 4) rows. Sleeve measures 5½ (6, 6½, 7, 7½, 8)" from beg. Finish off.

ASSEMBLY
Join shoulders: With RS of front and back together, sew 2¾ (3, 3¼, 3½, 3¾, 4)" from outside edge on each shoulder. Attach sleeves: Measure down 4½ (4½, 5, 5, 5½, 5½)" from shoulder seam on front and back and place markers. Sew in sleeves between markers. Sew side and underarm seams.

FINISHING
To form collar: Measure down 3½ (3½, 3½, 4, 4, 4)" from neck edge and place marker on each front edge. Turn back neck edge and tack into place.

To make cord for bow: With color B, attach yarn at marker on front and ch 25 (25, 28, 28, 30, 30). Work 1 sl st in second ch from hook and in each rem ch. Then sl st in hole at marker and finish off. Rep cord on other front edge.

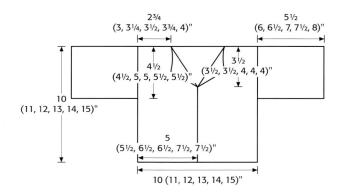

LITTLE BOY BLUE PULLOVER

He'll look just like Daddy in this white, denim blue, and navy pullover. Relaxed and oversized, this box-stitched sweater is sure to be one of his favorites.

SKILL LEVEL: ADVANCED BEGINNER

SIZES

Pullover: 6–12M (18M, 24M, 2T, 3T, 4T)

Finished Chest Measurement: 20 (22, 24, 26, 28, 30)"

MATERIALS

A 1 (2, 2, 3, 3, 3) balls Plymouth Wildflower DK (50g, 137yds/ball; 51% cotton, 49% acrylic), Navy 60

B 1 (2, 2, 3, 3, 3) balls Plymouth Wildflower DK, Denim Blue 10

C 1 (2, 2, 3, 3, 3) balls Plymouth Wildflower DK, White 41

Size 5.5 mm (I/9 US) crochet hook or size needed to obtain gauge

GAUGE

16 sts and 20 rows = 4" in sc

PULLOVER

FRONT AND BACK

With color A, ch 40 (44, 48, 52, 56, 60).

Row 1: Work 1 dc in third ch from hook and in each ch across, ch 2 (counts as first dc on following rows), turn— 39 (43, 47, 51, 55, 59) dc.

Row 2: Work 1 FPdc around each of next 2 dc, 1 BPdc around next dc, *1 FPdc around each of next 3 dc, 1 BPdc around next dc*; rep from * to * across to last 3 sts, work 1 FPdc around each of next 2 dc, 1 dc in turning ch-2 sp, ch 2, turn.

Row 3: Work 1 dc in next 2 dc, *1 FPdc around next BPdc, 1 dc in next 3 sts*; rep from * to * across to last 3 sts, work 1 dc in next 2 dc, 1 dc in turning ch-2 sp, ch 2, turn.

Row 4: Work 1 FPdc around each of next 2 dc, 1 BPdc around next dc, *1 FPdc around each of next 3 dc, 1 BPdc around next dc*; rep from * to * across to last 3 sts, work 1 FPdc around each of next 2 dc, 1 dc in turning ch-2 sp, ch 2, turn.

Row 5: Rep row 3.

Rep rows 4 and 5 for next 6 (6, 6, 8, 8, 10) rows—11 (11, 11, 13, 13, 15) total rows. At end of last row, change to color B.

Cont in patt, rep rows 4 and 5 for next 10 (10, 10, 12, 12, 14) rows. At end of last row, change to color C.

Cont in patt, rep rows 4 and 5 for next 8 (10, 10, 12, 12, 14) rows. At end of last row, do not ch 2. Finish off. Rep to make back.

SLEEVES (Make 2)
With color A, ch 36 (36, 40, 40, 44, 44).

Row 1: Work 1 dc in third ch from hook and in each ch across, ch 2 (counts as first dc on following rows), turn—35 (35, 39, 39, 43, 43) dc.

Row 2: Work 1 FPdc around each of the next 2 dc, 1 BPdc around next dc, *1 FPdc around each of next 3 dc, 1 BPdc around next dc*; rep from * to * across to last 3 sts. Work 1 FPdc around each of next 2 dc, 1 dc in turning ch-2 sp, ch 2, turn.

Row 3: Work 1 dc in next 2 dc, *1 FPdc around next BPdc, 1 dc in next 3 sts*; rep from * to * across to last 3 sts, work 1 dc in next 2 dc, 1 dc in turning ch-2 sp, ch 2, turn.

Row 4: Work 1 FPdc around each of next 2 dc, 1 BPdc around next dc, *1 FPdc around each of next 3 dc, 1 BPdc around next dc*; rep from * to * across to last 3 sts, work 1 FPdc around each of next 2 dc, 1 dc in turning ch-2 sp.

Row 5: Rep row 3.

Rep rows 4 and 5 for next 2 (2, 2, 4, 4, 4) rows—7 (7, 7, 9, 9, 9) total rows. At end of last row, change to color B.

Cont in patt, rep rows 4 and 5 for next 6 (6, 6, 8, 8, 8) rows. At end of last row, change to color C.

Cont in patt, rep rows 4 and 5 for next 6 (6, 6, 8, 8, 8) rows. At end of last row, do not ch 2. Finish off.

ASSEMBLY
Join shoulders: With RS of front and back together, sew 2½ (2¾, 3, 3½, 4, 4½)" from outside edge on each shoulder. Attach sleeves: Measure down 4½ (4½, 5, 5, 6, 6)" from shoulder seam on front and back and place markers. Sew sleeves between markers. Sew side and underarm seams.

FINISHING
With color B, work 2 rows sc evenly around neck edge.

With color B, work 31 (31, 35, 35, 39, 39) sc evenly around cuff. Work 1 more row of sc around cuff. Finish off.

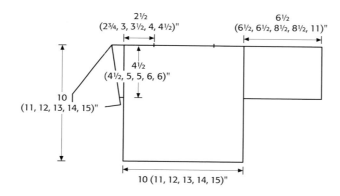

2½
(2¾, 3, 3½, 4, 4½)"

6½
(6½, 6½, 8½, 8½, 11)"

4½
(4½, 5, 5, 6, 6)"

10
(11, 12, 13, 14, 15)"

10 (11, 12, 13, 14, 15)"

COURT JESTER PULLOVER AND CAP

The purple trimmed headband, sleeves, and waistband on this whimsical ensemble enhance the lime green background. The shell stitch gives a soft scalloped edge to the sleeves and waistband.

SIZES

Pullover: 6–12M (18M, 24M, 2T, 3T, 4T)

Finished Chest Measurement: 21 (24, 24, 28, 28, 31)"

Cap: Small (Medium, Large)

Circumference: 17 (19, 21)"

MATERIALS

A 4 (4, 5, 5, 6, 7) balls Plymouth Wildflower DK (50g, 137yds/ball; 51% cotton, 49% acrylic), Lime 58

B 1 (2, 2, 2, 2, 3) balls Plymouth Wildflower DK, Purple 45

Size 5.5 mm (I/9 US) crochet hook or size needed to obtain gauge

GAUGE

16 sts and 20 rows = 4" in sc

PULLOVER

The front and back are worked from the top down.

FRONT AND BACK

With color A, ch 38 (44, 44, 50, 50, 56).

Row 1: Work 2 sc in second ch from hook, 1 sc in each ch across, ch 1, turn—37 (43, 43, 49, 49, 55) sc.

Row 2: Work 1 sc in next sc, *sk next 2 sc, work 7 dc in next sc, sk next 2 sc, work 1 sc in next sc*; rep from * to * across, ch 3, turn—6 (7, 7, 8, 8, 9) shells.

Row 3: Work 3 dc in next sc, *sk next 3 sts, work 1 sc in next dc, sk next 3 sts, work 7 dc in next sc*; rep from * to * another 4 (5, 5, 6, 6, 7) times, sk next 3 sts, work 1 sc in next dc, sk next 3 sts, work 4 dc in last sc, ch 1, turn—1 half shell, 5 (6, 6, 7, 7, 8) shells, and 1 half shell.

Row 4: Work 1 sc in next dc, *sk next 3 sts, work 7 dc in next sc, sk next 3 sts, work 1 sc in next dc*; rep from * to * across, ch 3, turn—6 (7, 7, 8, 8, 9) shells.

Rep rows 3 and 4 until front measures 8 (8, 9, 9, 10, 10)".

Change to color B and rep rows 3 and 4 another 2 (3, 3, 4, 4, 5) times. Front measures 10 (11, 12, 13, 14, 15)" from beg. Finish off. Rep to make back.

SLEEVES (Make 2)
With color A, ch 38 (38, 38, 44, 44, 44).

Row 1: Work 1 sc in second ch from hook and in each ch across, ch 1, turn—37 (37, 37, 43, 43, 43) sc.

Row 2: Work 1 sc in first sc, * sk next 2 sc, work 7 dc in next sc, sk next 2 sc, work 1 sc in next sc*; rep from * to * across, ch 3, turn—6 (6, 6, 7, 7, 7) shells.

Row 3: Work 3 dc in first sc, *sk next 3 sts, work 1 sc in next dc, sk next 3 sts, work 7 dc in next sc*; rep from * to * another 4 (4, 4, 5, 5, 5) times, sk next 3 sts, work 1 sc in next dc, sk next 3 sts, work 4 dc in last sc, ch 1, turn—1 half shell, 5 (5, 5, 6, 6, 6) shells, and 1 half shell.

Row 4: Work 1 sc in first dc, *sk next 3 sts, work 7 dc in next sc, sk next 3 sts, work 1 sc in next dc*; rep from * to * across, ch 3, turn—6 (6, 6, 7, 7, 7) shells.

Rep rows 3 and 4 until sleeve measures 5 (5½, 6, 6, 6½, 6½)" from beg.

Change to color B and rep rows 3 and 4 another 2 (2, 2, 3, 3, 3) times. Sleeve measures 6½ (7, 7½, 8¼, 8¾, 8¾)" from beg.

ASSEMBLY
Join shoulders: With RS of front and back together, sew 1½ (2, 2½, 3, 3, 3)" from outside edge on each shoulder. Attach sleeves: Measure down 5 (5, 5, 6, 6, 6)" from shoulder seam on front and back and place markers. Sew in sleeves between markers. Sew side and underarm seams.

CAP

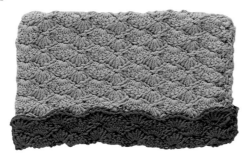

PANEL
With color A, ch 32 (38, 44).

Row 1: Work 1 sc in second ch from hook, 1 sc in each ch across, ch 1, turn—31 (37, 43) sc.

Row 2: Work 1 sc in first sc, *sk next 2 sc, work 7 dc in next sc, sk next 2 sc, work 1 sc in next sc*; rep from * to * across, ch 3, turn—5 (6, 7) shells.

Row 3: Work 3 dc in first sc, *sk next 3 sts, work 1 sc in next dc, sk next 3 sts, work 7 dc in next sc*; rep from * to* another 3 (4, 5) times, sk next 3 sts, work 1 sc in next dc, sk next 3 sts, work 4 dc in last sc, ch 1, turn—1 half shell, 4 (5, 6) shells, and 1 half shell.

Row 4: Work 1 sc in first dc, *sk next 3 sts, work 7 dc in next sc, sk next 3 sts, work 1 sc in next dc*; rep from * to * across, ch 3, turn—5 (6, 7) shells.

Rep rows 3 and 4 another 10 (12, 14) times.

Change to color B and rep rows 3 and 4 another 2 (3, 3) times. Finish off.

Attach color B to beg of cap and work across frlps as follows: Work 1 sc in first frlp, *sk next 2 frlps, work 7 dc in next frlp, sk next 2 frlps, work 1 sc in next frlp*; rep from * to * across, ch 3, turn—5 (6, 7) shells.

Rep rows 3 and 4 another 1 (2, 2) times. Finish off.

ASSEMBLY
With RS facing, fold cap panel in half widthwise. Sew sides from fold to edge of color B (brim). Turn cap RS out. Sew sides of color B (brim). Fold brim back to crown and sew brim to crown through both thicknesses.

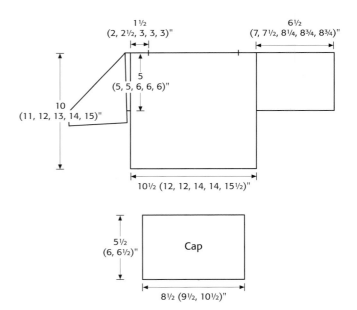

PALM BEACH CARDIGAN

Nothing says sunny days like the Palm Beach cardigan. Crocheted in a cluster stitch, this crisp white cardigan has short sleeves and a turned collar. It's a fast and fun project.

SIZES

Cardigan: 6–12M (18M, 24M, 2T, 3T, 4T)

Finished Chest Measurement: 20 (22, 24, 26, 28, 30)"

MATERIALS

3 (3, 4, 4, 5, 5) balls Plymouth Wildflower DK (50g, 137yds/ball; 51% cotton, 49% acrylic), White 41

Size 5.5 mm (I/9 US) crochet hook or size needed to obtain gauge

1½"-diameter decorative button

GAUGE

16 sts and 20 rows = 4" in sc

CARDIGAN

BACK

Ch 44 (48, 52, 56, 60, 64).

Row 1: Work 3 dc in fourth ch from hook, *sk next 3 chs, work (1 sc, ch 3, 3 dc) in next ch*; rep from * to * across to last 4 chs, sk next 3 chs, work 1 sc in last ch, ch 3, turn.

Row 2: Work 3 dc in first sc, *work (1 sc, ch 3, 3 dc) in next ch-3 sp*; rep from * to * across to last ch-3 sp, work 1 sc in last ch-3 sp, ch 3, turn.

Rep row 2 until back measures 10 (11, 12, 13, 14, 15)" from beg. Finish off.

FRONT (Make 2)

Ch 24 (24, 28, 28, 32, 32).

Row 1: Work 3 dc in fourth ch from hook, *sk next 3 chs, work (1 sc, ch 3, 3 dc) in next ch*; rep from * to * across to last 4 chs, sk next 3 chs, work 1 sc in last ch, ch 3, turn.

Row 2: Work 3 dc in first sc, *work (1 sc, ch 3, 3 dc) in next ch-3 sp*; rep from * to * across to last ch-3 sp, work 1 sc in last ch-3 sp, ch 3, turn.

Rep row 2 until front measures 10 (11, 12, 13, 14, 15)" from beg. Finish off.

SLEEVES (Make 2)

Ch 40 (40, 40, 44, 44, 44).

Row 1: Work 3 dc in fourth ch from hook, *sk next 3 chs, work (1 sc, ch 3, 3 dc) in next ch*; rep from * to * across to last 4 chs, sk next 3 chs, work 1 sc in last ch, ch 3, turn.

Row 2: Work 3 dc in first sc, *work (1 sc, ch 3, 3 dc) in next ch-3 sp*; rep from * to * across to last ch-3 sp, work 1 sc in last ch-3 sp, ch 3, turn.

Rep row 2 until sleeve measures 3½ (3½, 4, 4, 4½, 4½)" from beg. Finish off.

ASSEMBLY

Join shoulders: With RS of front and back together, sew 2¾ (3, 3, 3¼, 3½, 4)" from outside edge on each shoulder. Attach sleeves: Measure down 4½ (4½, 4½, 5, 5, 5)" from shoulder seam on front and back and place markers. Sew in sleeves between markers. Sew side and underarm seams.

FINISHING

To form collar: Measure down 3½ (3½, 3½, 4, 4, 4)" from neck edge and place marker on each front panel. Turn back neck edge and tack into place.

On left front, attach button at marker. Use a loose stitch on right front as buttonhole.

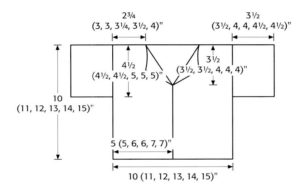

PEACE AND LOVE PICNIC DRESS AND SCARF

This is the perfect outfit for sunny days filled with parties, backyard barbecues, or lounging in a hammock. Lime green, celadon green, and aqua blue are worked in a zigzag stitch to make this a fun and easy project. Best of all, it is made entirely of single crochet.

SKILL LEVEL: ADVANCED BEGINNER

SIZES

Dress: 6–12M (18–24M, 2T–3T, 4T)

Finished Chest Measurement: 22½ (27, 31½, 36)"

Scarf Measurements: 10 (11, 12, 13)" wide (not including ties) 7½" (8½, 9½, 10½)" long

MATERIALS

A 2 (3, 3, 4) balls Plymouth Wildflower DK (50g, 137yds/ball; 51% cotton, 49% acrylic), Lime Green 58

B 2 (2, 3, 4) balls Plymouth Wildflower DK, Aqua Blue 55

C 1 (2, 2, 3) balls Plymouth Wildflower DK, Celadon Green 19

Size 5.5 mm (I/9 US) crochet hook or size needed to obtain gauge

GAUGE

16 sts and 20 rows = 4" in sc

This pattern is designed for row counting; an accurate gauge is essential!

DRESS

FRONT AND BACK
With color A, ch 73 (87, 101, 115).

Row 1: Work 1 sc in third ch from hook, 1 sc in next 5 ch, *sk next 3 ch, work 1 sc in next 5 ch, 3 sc in next ch, 1 sc in next 5 ch*; rep from * to * across to last 9 ch, sk next 3 ch, work 1 sc in next 5 ch, 2 sc in last ch, ch 1, turn.

Row 2: Work 1 sc in first sc, 1 sc in next 5 sc, *sk next 2 sc, work 1 sc in next 5 sc, 3 sc in next sc, 1 sc in next 5 sc*; rep from * to * across to last 7 sts, sk next 2 sc, work 1 sc in next 4 sc, 3 sc in last sc. At end of row, change to color B, ch 1, turn.

Row 3: With color B, rep row 2.

Row 4: With color B, rep row 2. At end of row, change to color C, ch 1, turn.

Row 5: With color C, work 1 sc in first sc in front lp only, 1 sc in next 5 sc in front lps only, *sk next 2 sc, work 1 sc in next 5 sc in front lps only, 3 sc in next sc in front lps only, 1 sc in next 5 sc in front lps only*; rep from * to * across to last 7 sts, sk next 2 sc, work 1 sc in next 4 sc, 3 sc in last sc, ch 1, turn.

Row 6: With color C, rep row 2. At end of row, change to color A, ch 1, turn.

Row 7: With color A, rep row 2.

Rep rows 2–7 another 7 (8, 9, 10) times.

Next row: With color A, rep row 2. Finish off.

Rep to make back.

ASSEMBLY
With RS of front and back facing, measure 3½ (4, 4½, 5)" down from top on both sides and place marker. Sew side seams from marker to bottom edge. Turn dress RS out.

FINISHING
Shoulder straps: Attach color B to top corner of front, work 2 sc in first sc, sk next 10 sc, *work 1 sc in next 3 sc, sk next 10 sc*; rep from * to *, end with 2 sc in last sc. Ch 12 (16, 18, 22). Work 2 sc in first sc of back, sk next 10 sc, *work 1 sc in next 3 sc, sk next 10 sc*; rep from * to *, end with 2 sc in last sc. Ch 14 (16, 18, 22). Attach ch to beg st on front with sl st. Next row: Sl st in each sc around. Finish off.

SCARF

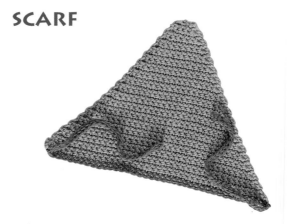

With color A, ch 3.

Row 1: Work 1 sc in second ch from hook, 1 sc in next ch, ch 1, turn.

Row 2: Work 2 sc in first sc, 1 sc in each sc across, ch 1, turn.

Row 3: Rep row 2 until scarf measures 10 (11, 12, 13)" across. Finish off.

Next row: With color B, ch 30. Attach yarn to last st worked in scarf with 1 sc and work 1 sc in each sc across, ch 30, turn.

Final row: Sl st in each ch and sc across. Finish off.

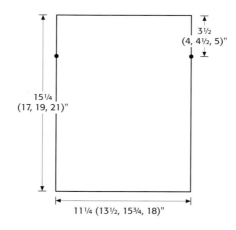

15¼ (17, 19, 21)"

3½ (4, 4½, 5)"

11¼ (13½, 15¾, 18)"

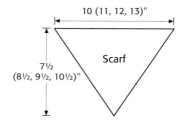

10 (11, 12, 13)"

7½ (8½, 9½, 10½)"

Scarf

Seaside Pullover with Hood

Warm days and cool nights call for the Seaside sweater. This relaxed, hooded pullover is done in a texture stitch and a soft salmon color. It's just right for an evening or afternoon spent lounging.

SIZES

Pullover: 6–12M (18M, 24M, 2T, 3T, 4T)

Finished Chest Measurement: 20 (22, 24, 26, 28, 30)"

MATERIALS

4 (5, 6, 6, 7, 8) balls Plymouth Wildflower DK (50g, 137yds/ball; 51% cotton, 49% acrylic), Salmon 13

Size 5.5 mm (I/9 US) crochet hook or size needed to obtain gauge

GAUGE

16 sts and 20 rows = 4" in sc

PULLOVER

FRONT AND BACK

Ch 37 (41, 45, 49, 53, 57).

Row 1: Work 1 sc in second ch from hook, 1 dc in next ch, *1 sc in next ch, 1 dc in next ch*; rep from * to * across, ch 1, turn—36 (40, 44, 48, 52, 56) sts.

Row 2: Work 1 sc in first dc, 1 dc in next sc, *1 sc in next dc, 1 dc in next sc*; rep from * to * across, ch 1, turn.

Rep row 2 until front measures 10 (11, 12, 13, 14, 15)" from beg. Finish off. Rep to make back.

SLEEVES (Make 2)

Ch 25 (27, 29, 31, 31, 31).

Row 1: Work 1 sc in second ch from hook, 1 dc in next ch, *1 sc in next ch, 1 dc in next ch*; rep from * to * across, ch 1, turn—24 (26, 28, 30, 30, 30) sts.

Row 2: Work 1 sc in first dc, 1 dc in next sc, *1 sc in next dc, 1 dc in next sc*; rep from * to * across, ch 1, turn.

Row 3: Work (1 sc, 1 dc, 1 sc) in first dc, 1 dc in next sc, *1 sc in next dc, 1 dc in next sc*; rep from * to * across, ch 1, turn—26 (28, 30, 32, 32, 32) sts.

Rows 4 and 5: Work 1 sc in first dc, 1 dc in next sc, *1 sc in next dc, 1 dc in next sc*; rep from * to * across, ch 1, turn.

Row 6: Work (1 sc, 1 dc, 1 sc) in first dc, 1 dc in next sc, *1 sc in next dc, 1 dc in next sc*; rep from * to * across, ch 1, turn—28 (30, 32, 34, 34, 34) sts.

Rep rows 4–6 until sleeve measures 6½ (7, 7½, 8, 9, 10)" from beg. Finish off.

HOOD

Ch 49 (53, 57, 59, 61, 63).

Row 1: Work 1 sc in second ch from hook, 1 dc in next ch, *1 sc in next ch, 1 dc in next ch*; rep from * to * across, ch 1, turn—48 (52, 56, 58, 60, 62) sts.

Row 2: Work 1 sc in first dc, 1 dc in next sc, *1 sc in next dc, 1 dc in next sc*; rep from * to * across, ch 1, turn.

Rep row 2 until hood measures 7½ (8, 8½, 8¾, 9, 9¼)" from beg. Finish off.

ASSEMBLY

With RS of front and back together, st 2½ (2¾, 3, 3½, 4, 4½)" from outside edge on each shoulder. Measure down 5 (5½, 6, 6½, 7, 7½)" from shoulder seam on front and back and place markers. Sew in sleeves between markers. Sew side and underarm seams. Fold hood in half with RS together and stitch top seam as shown below. Turn RS out. Evenly space hood around neck edge and sew into place, ending at center front.

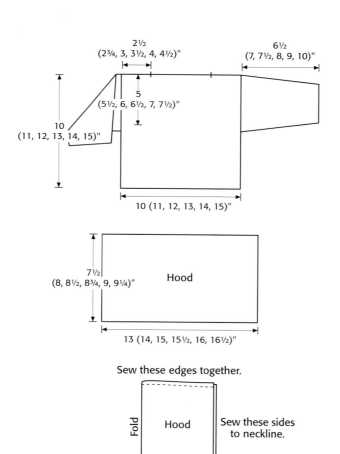

PATRIOT GAMES DRESS
AND BERET

Show your spirit in this adorable Americana ensemble. Scallop-stitched skirt, red-and-white striped, three-quarter-length sleeves, and a coordinating beret will have your favorite little girl dressed to impress.

SIZES

Size: 6–12M (18–24M, 2T, 3T, 4T)

Finished Chest Measurement: 20 (22, 24, 26, 28)"

Beret: Small (Medium, Large)

Circumference: 17 (19, 21)"

MATERIALS

A 2 (3, 3, 3, 4) balls Plymouth Wildflower DK (50g, 137yds/ball; 51% cotton, 49% acrylic), Denim Blue 10

B 2 (2, 2, 3, 3) balls Plymouth Wildflower DK, White 41

C 1 ball Plymouth Wildflower DK, Bright Red

Size 5.5 mm (I/9 US) crochet hook or size needed to obtain gauge

GAUGE

16 sts and 20 rows = 4" in sc

DRESS

The dress is made by crocheting the skirt panels first from the waist down, then attaching yarn to the waist of each skirt panel and working up to the shoulder.

SKIRT PANELS (Make 2)
With color A, ch 42 (46, 50, 54, 58).

Row 1: Work 1 sc in second ch from hook and in each ch across, ch 1, turn—41 (45, 49, 53, 57) sc.

Row 2: Work 1 sc in first sc, *sk next sc, work 3 dc in next sc, sk next sc, work 1 sc in next sc*; rep from * to * across, ch 3, turn—10 (11, 12, 13, 14) shells.

Row 3: Work 1 dc in first sc, *sk next dc, work 1 sc in next dc, sk next dc, work 3 dc in next sc*; rep from * to * across, end last rep with 2 dc in last sc, ch 1, turn—1 half shell, 9 (10, 11, 12, 13) shells, 1 half shell.

Row 4: Work 1 sc in first dc, *sk next dc, work 3 dc in next sc, sk next dc, work 1 sc in next dc*; rep from * to * across, ch 3, turn.

Rep rows 3 and 4 until skirt measures 9 (10, 11, 12, 13)" from beg. Finish off.

BODICE BACK

With color B, join yarn to top of skirt and work 40 (44, 48, 52, 56) sc evenly across row.

Row 1: Work 1 sc in each sc across, ch 1, turn.

Rep row 1 until bodice back measures 6 (6¼, 6½, 6¾, 7)" from beg. Finish off.

BODICE FRONT

Work as for back until bodice front measures 4 (4¼, 4½, 4¼, 4½)" from beg. Beg neck shaping.

NECK SHAPING

Work both sides at same time.

Next row: Work 1 sc in next 15 (17, 19, 20, 22) sc, sk next 10 (10, 10, 12,12) sc. With a second ball of yarn, work 1 sc in rem 15 (17, 19, 20, 22) sc.

Next 4 (4, 4, 5, 5) rows: Work across each row, dec 1 sc at neck edge—11 (13, 15, 15, 17) sts rem on each side.

Rep row 2 until bodice front measures 6 (6¼, 6½, 6¾, 7)" from beg. Finish off.

SLEEVES (Make 2)

With color C, ch 25 (27, 29, 31, 33).

Row 1: Work 1 sc in second ch from hook and in each ch across, ch 1, turn—24 (26, 28, 30, 32) sc.

Rows 2 and 3: Work 1 sc in each sc across, ch 1, turn.

Row 4: Work 1 sc in each sc across. At end of row, change to color B, ch 1, turn.

Rows 5, 6, and 7: Rep row 2.

Row 8: Work 1 sc in each sc across. At end of row, change to color C, ch 1, turn.

Rep rows 1–8 another 2 (2, 3, 3, 3) times, alternating colors. Finish off.

STAR (Make 2)

With color C, ch 2.

Rnd 1: Work 5 sc in second ch from hook—5 sc.

Rnd 2: Work 3 sc in each sc around—15 sc.

Rnd 3: *Work 1 sc in next sc, (1 hdc, 1 dc, 1 hdc) in next sc, 1 sc in next sc*; rep from * to * around—25 sts.

Rnd 4: *Sl st in next sc, work 1 sc in next hdc, ch 2, work 1 dc in next dc, ch 2, work 1 sc in next hdc, 1 sl st in next sc*; rep from * to * around. Finish off.

ASSEMBLY

Join shoulders: With RS of front and back together, sew 2¾ (3¼, 3½, 3¾, 4½)" from outside edge on each shoulder. Attach sleeves: Measure down 4 (4¼, 4½, 4¾, 5)" from shoulder seam on front and back and place markers. Sew in sleeves between markers. Sew side and underarm seams.

FINISHING

With color A, work 2 rows sc evenly around neck edge.

Center star on bodice and sew into place.

BERET

TOP

Sizes Small and Medium: Do not work rnds 19 and 20.

Note: Mark beg of rnds. Rnds are worked continuously; do not join.

With color A, ch 2.

Rnd 1: Work 6 sc in second ch from hook.

Rnd 2: Work 2 sc in each sc around—12 sc.

Rnd 3: *Work 1 sc in next sc, 2 sc in next sc*; rep from * to * 6 times—18 sc.

Rnd 4: *Work 1 sc in next sc, 2 sc in next sc*; rep from * to * 9 times—27 sc.

Rnd 5: *Work 1 sc in next 2 sc, 2 sc in next sc*; rep from * to * 9 times—36 sc.

Rnds 6, 8, 10, 12, 14, 16, and 18: Work 1 sc in each sc around.

Rnd 7: *Work 1 sc in next 3 sc, 2 sc in next sc*; rep from * to * 9 times—45 sc.

Rnd 9: *Work 1 sc in next 4 sc, 2 sc in next sc*; rep from * to * 9 times—54 sc.

Rnd 11: *Work 1 sc in next 5 sc, 2 sc in next sc*; rep from * to * 9 times—63 sc.

Rnd 13: *Work 1 sc in next 6 sc, 2 sc in next sc*; rep from * to * 9 times—72 sc.

Rnd 15: *Work 1 sc in next 7 sc, 2 sc in next sc*; rep from * to * 9 times—81 sc.

Rnd 17: *Work 1 sc in next 8 sc, 2 sc in next sc*; rep from * to * 9 times—90 sc.

Rnd 19: *Work 1 sc in next 9 sc, 2 sc in next sc*; rep from * to * 9 times—99 sc.

Rnd 20: Work 1 sc in each sc around. Finish off.

BOTTOM

Small: Complete rnds 1–7.

Medium: Sk rnds 2, 3, 8, and 9.

Large: Sk rnds 2–5.

With color A, ch 64 (72, 81). Join first and last lps in ch with sl st.

Rnd 1: Work 1 sc in each ch around.

Rnd 2: *Work 1 sc in next 6 sc, 2 sc in next sc*; rep from * to * 9 times—72 sc.

Rnds 3, 5, and 7: Work 1 sc in each sc around.

Rnd 4: *Work 1 sc in next 7 sc, 2 sc in next sc*; rep from * to * 9 times—81 sc.

Rnd 6: *Work 1 sc in next 8 sc, 2 sc in next sc*; rep from * to * 9 times—90 sc.

Rnd 8: *Work 1 sc in next 9 sc, 2 sc in next sc*; rep from * to * 9 times—99 sc.

Rnd 9: Work 1 sc in each sc around. Finish off.

ASSEMBLY

With WS together, join top and bottom pieces by working sc in each sc around outside edge. Finish off.

FINISHING

With color A, join yarn to bottom inside edge, work 4 rnds sc evenly around edge of headband. Finish off.

Attach star to front of hat (see photo for placement).

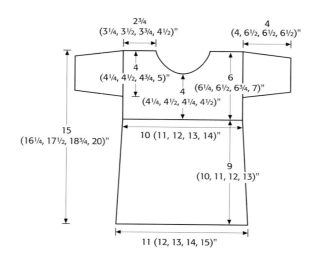

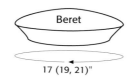

ORANGE MARMALADE PULLOVER AND CHAPEAU

First signs of fall—colors of olive oil, paprika, and periwinkle—were combined to make the Orange Marmalade ensemble. This relaxed pullover and oversized hat are trimmed in a faux-fur texture stitch.

SKILL LEVEL: ADVANCED BEGINNER

SIZES

Pullover: 6–12M (18M, 24M, 2T, 3T, 4T)

Finished Chest Measurement: 20 (22, 24, 26, 28, 30)"

Chapeau: Small (Medium, Large)

Circumference: 16 (18, 20)"

MATERIALS

A 1 (1, 2, 2, 3, 3) balls Plymouth Wildflower DK (50g, 137yds/ball; 51% cotton, 49% acrylic), Periwinkle 74

B 1 ball Plymouth Wildflower DK, Paprika 73

C 4 (4, 5, 6, 8, 9) balls Plymouth Wildflower DK, Olive Oil 76

Size 5.5 mm (I/9 US) crochet hook or size needed to obtain gauge

GAUGE

16 sts and 20 rows = 4" in sc

PULLOVER

BACK

With color A, ch 41 (45, 49, 53, 57, 61).

Row 1: Work 1 sc in second ch from hook and in each ch across, ch 1, turn—40 (44, 48, 52, 56, 60) sc.

Rows 2, 4, and 6: *Ch 5, working in back lp only, work 1 sl st in next sc, inserting hook from back to front*; rep from * to * across to last st, ch 5, work 1 sc in last st, ch 1, turn.

Rows 3 and 5: Work 1 sc in each sc across, ch 1, turn.

Row 7: Work 1 sc in each sc across, at end of row, change to color B, ch 1, turn.

Row 8: Work 1 sc in each sc across, ch 1, turn.

Row 9: Work 1 sc in back lp only of each sc across, at end of row, change to color C, ch 1, turn.

Row 10: Work 1 sc in front lp only of each sc across, ch 1, turn.

Row 11: Work 1 sc in each sc across, ch 1, turn.

Rep row 11 until back measures 10 (11, 12, 13, 14, 15)" from beg. Finish off.

FRONT

Work as for back until front measures 8 (9, 9¾, 10¾, 11½, 12½)" from beg. Beg neck shaping.

NECK SHAPING

Row 1: Work 1 sc in first 13 (15, 16, 18, 20, 21) sc, ch 1, turn.

Row 2: Dec 1 sc over first 2 sc, work 1 sc in each sc across, ch 1, turn.

Row 3: Work 1 sc in each sc across, ch 1, turn.

Rep rows 2 and 3 another 3 times.

Rep row 3 until front measures 10 (11, 12, 13, 14, 15)" from beg. Finish off.

Join yarn to opposite shoulder and rep neck shaping. Finish off.

SLEEVES (Make 2)

With color A, ch 31 (31, 33, 33, 35, 35).

Row 1: Work 1 sc in second ch from hook and in each ch across, ch 1, turn—30 (30, 32, 32, 34, 34) sc.

Rows 2, 4, and 6: *Ch 5, work 1 sl st in back lp only of next sc, inserting hook from back to front*; rep from * to * across to last st, ch 5, work 1 sc in last st, ch 1, turn.

Rows 3 and 5: Work 1 sc in each sc across, ch 1, turn.

Row 7: Work 1 sc in each sc across, at end of row, change to color B, ch 1, turn.

Row 8: Work 1 sc in each sc across, ch 1, turn.

Row 9: Work 1 sc in back lp only of each sc across, at end of row, change to color C, ch 1, turn.

Row 10: Work 1 sc in front lp only of each sc across, ch 1, turn.

Row 11: Work 2 sc in first sc, 1 sc in each sc across, 2 sc in last sc, ch 1, turn—32 (32, 34, 34, 36, 36) sc.

Rows 12–15: Work 1 sc in each sc across, ch 1, turn.

Row 16: Work 2 sc in first sc, 1 sc in each sc across, 2 sc in last sc, ch 1, turn—34 (34, 36, 36, 38, 38) sc.

Rep rows 12–16 until sleeve measures 6½ (7½, 8½, 9½, 10½, 11½)" from beg. Finish off.

ASSEMBLY

Join shoulders: With RS of front and back together, sew 3 (3½, 4, 4¼, 4¾, 5)" from outside edge on each shoulder. Attach sleeves: Measure down 5 (5, 5½, 5½, 6, 6)" from shoulder seam on front and back and place markers. Sew in sleeves between markers. Sew side and underarm seams.

FINISHING

Trim

With color B, work 1 row sc evenly around neck edge. Finish off.

Popcorn Buttons

Find center of front and measure down 1" from neck edge. With color A, attach yarn to fp. In the same fp, work 1 sc, 5 dc, 1 sc. Insert hook through first sc of button, sl st, and finish off. Measure down another 1" and rep to make second button. Finish off.

CHAPEAU

Small: Complete rnds 1–18, 22–26, and 34–46.

Medium: Complete all rnds except 21, 31, 32, and 37.

Large: Complete all rnds except 36 and 37.

Rnd 1: With color C, ch 2, work 6 sc in second ch from hook.

Rnd 2: Work 1 sc in first sc, 2 sc in each sc around, join with sl st to first sc, ch 1—11 sc.

Rnd 3: Work 2 sc in each sc; rep 11 times, join with sl st to first sc, ch 1—22 sc.

Rnds 4, 6, 8, 10, 12, 14, 16, 18, and 20: Work 1 sc in each sc around, join with sl st to first sc, ch 1.

Rnd 5: *Work 1 sc in next sc, 2 sc in next sc*; rep from * to * 11 times, join with sl st to first sc, ch 1—33 sc.

Rnd 7: *Work 1 sc in next 2 sc, 2 sc in next sc*; rep from * to * 11 times, join with sl st to first sc, ch 1—44 sc.

Rnd 9: *Work 1 sc in next 3 sc, 2 sc in next sc*; rep from * to * 11 times, join with sl st to first sc, ch 1—55 sc.

Rnd 11: *Work 1 sc in next 4 sc, 2 sc in next sc*; rep from * to * 11 times, join with sl st to first sc, ch 1—66 sc.

Rnd 13: *Work 1 sc in next 5 sc, 2 sc in next sc*; rep from * to * 11 times, join with sl st to first sc, ch 1—77 sc.

Rnd 15: *Work 1 sc in next 6 sc, 2 sc in next sc*; rep from * to * 11 times, join with sl st to first sc, ch 1—88 sc.

Rnd 17: *Work 1 sc in next 7 sc, 2 sc in next sc*; rep from * to * 11 times, join with sl st to first sc, ch 1—99 sc.

Rnd 19: *Work 1 sc in next 8 sc, 2 sc in next sc*; rep from * to * 11 times, join with sl st to first sc, ch 1—110 sc.

Rnd 21: *Work 1 sc in next 9 sc, 2 sc in next sc*; rep from * to * 11 times, join with sl st to first sc, ch 1—121 sc.

Rnds 22–30: Work 1 sc in each sc around, join with sl st to first sc, ch 1.

Rnd 31: *Work 1 sc in next 9 sc, dec 1 sc over next 2 sc*; rep from * to * 11 times, join with sl st to first sc, ch 1—110 sc.

Rnd 32: Work 1 sc in each sc around, join with sl st to first sc, ch 1.

Rnd 33: *Work 1 sc in next 8 sc, dec 1 sc over next 2 sc*; rep from * to * 11 times, join with sl st to first sc, ch 1—99 sc.

Rnd 34–37: *Work 1 sc in next 9 sc, dec 1 sc over next 2 sc*; rep from * to * 9 times, join with sl st to first sc, ch 1—90 sc. Cont to work rnds, dec the number of sc you work in by 1 for each of the 9 repeats in each rnd. You will dec total number of sc by 9 on each rnd—63 sc at end of rnd 37.

Rnd 38: Change to color B, work 1 sc in each sc around, join with sl st to first sc, ch 1.

Rnd 39: In back lps only, work 1 sc in each sc around, join with sl st to first sc, change to color A.

Rnd 40: In back lps only, work 1 sc in each sc around, join with sl st to first sc.

Rnd 41: *Ch 5, work 1 sl st in back lps only of next sc, inserting hook from back to front*; rep from * to * around, join with sl st to first sc, ch 1, turn.

Rnd 42: Work 1 sc in each sc around, ch 1, turn.

Rnds 43–46: Rep rnds 41 and 42 another 2 times. Finish off.

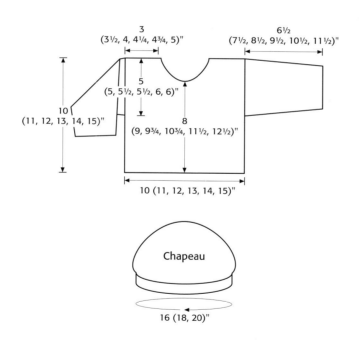

Baby's Bubble Pullover and Beret

Step out in style in this very chic pullover and beret. Celadon green bubbles accent a soft lavender background. This set is made entirely of single crochet stitches!

SIZES

Pullover: 6–12M (18M, 24M, 2T, 3T, 4T)

Finished Chest Measurement: 20 (22, 24, 26, 28, 30)"

Beret: Small (Medium, Large)

Circumference: 17 (19, 21)"

MATERIALS

A 4 (4, 5, 6, 7, 8) balls Plymouth Wildflower DK (50g, 137yds/ball; 51% cotton, 49% acrylic), Lavender 50

B 1 ball Plymouth Wildflower DK, Celadon Green 19

Size 5.5 mm (I/9 US) crochet hook or size needed to obtain gauge

GAUGE

16 sts and 20 rows = 4" in sc

PULLOVER

BACK

With color A, ch 41 (45, 49, 53, 57, 61).

Row 1: Work 1 sc in second ch from hook and in each ch across, ch 1, turn—40 (44, 48, 52, 56, 60) sc.

Row 2: Work 1 sc in each sc across, ch 1, turn.

Rep row 2 until back measures 9½ (10½, 11½, 12½, 13½, 14½)" from beg. Finish off.

FRONT

Work as for back until front measures 7½ (8½, 9½, 10½, 11½, 12½)" from beg. Beg neck shaping.

NECK SHAPING

Work both sides at same time.

Next row: Work 1 sc in first 15 (17, 19, 20, 22, 24) sc, sk next 10 (10, 10, 12, 12, 12) sc. With a second ball of yarn, work 1 sc in rem 15 (17, 19, 20, 22, 24) sc.

Next 4 (4, 4, 5, 5, 5) rows: Work across each row, dec 1 sc at neck edge—11 (13, 15, 15, 17, 19) sc rem on each side.

Rep row 2 until front measures 9½ (10½, 11½, 12½, 13½, 14½)" from beg. Finish off.

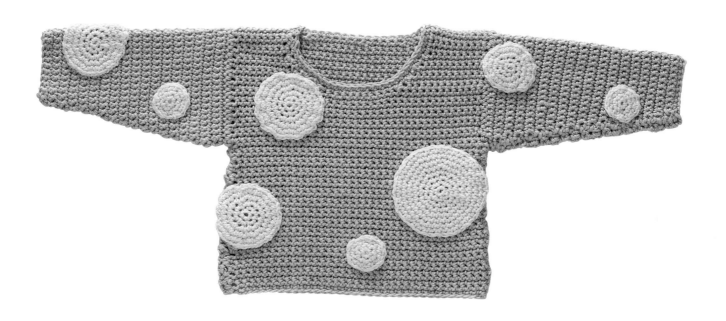

SLEEVES (Make 2)

With color A, ch 25 (27, 29, 31, 33, 35).

Row 1: Work 1 sc in second ch from hook and in each sc across, ch 1, turn—24 (26, 28, 30, 32, 34) sc.

Rows 2, 3, and 4: Work 1 sc in each sc across, ch 1, turn.

Row 5: Work 2 sc in first sc, 1 sc in each sc across, 2 sc in last sc, ch 1, turn—26 (28, 30, 32, 34, 36) sc.

Rep rows 1–5 until sleeve measures 6 (7, 8, 9, 10, 11)" from beg—36 (40, 44, 48, 52, 56) sc. Finish off.

ASSEMBLY

Join shoulders: With RS of front and back together, sew 2¾ (3¼, 3½, 3¾, 4½, 4½)" from outside edge on each shoulder. Attach sleeves: Measure down 4½ (5, 5½, 6, 6½, 7)" from shoulder seam on front and back and place markers. Sew in sleeves between markers. Sew side and underarm seams.

FINISHING

With color A, work 2 rows sc evenly around neck edge.

BERET

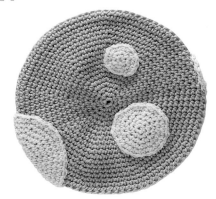

TOP

Small and Medium: Do not work rnds 19 and 20.

Note: Mark beg of rnds. Rnds are worked continuously; do not join.

With color A, ch 2.

Rnd 1: Work 6 sc in 2nd ch from hook.

Rnd 2: Work 2 sc in each sc around—12 sc.

Rnd 3: *Work 1 sc in next sc, 2 sc in next sc*; rep from * to * 6 times—18 sc.

Rnd 4: *Work 1 sc in next sc, 2 sc in next sc*; rep from * to * 9 times—27 sc.

Rnd 5: *Work 1 sc in next 2 sc, 2 sc in next sc*; rep from * to * 9 times—36 sc.

Rnds 6, 8, 10, 12, 14, 16, and 18: Work 1 sc in each sc around.

Rnd 7: *Work 1 sc in next 3 sc, 2 sc in next sc*; rep from * to * 9 times—45 sc.

Rnd 9: *Work 1 sc in next 4 sc, 2 sc in next sc*; rep from * to * 9 times—54 sc.

Rnd 11: *Work 1 sc in next 5 sc, 2 sc in next sc*; rep from * to * 9 times—63 sc.

Rnd 13: *Work 1 sc in next 6 sc, 2 sc in next sc*; rep from * to * 9 times—72 sc.

Rnd 15: *Work 1 sc in next 7 sc, 2 sc in next sc*; rep from * to * 9 times—81 sc.

Rnd 17: *Work 1 sc in next 8 sc, 2 sc in next sc*; rep from * to * 9 times—90 sc.

Rnd 19: *Work 1 sc in next 9 sc, 2 sc in next sc*; rep from * to * 9 times—99 sc.

Rnd 20: Work 1 sc in each sc around. Finish off.

BOTTOM

Small: Complete all rnds except 8 and 9.

Medium: Sk rnds 2, 3, 8, and 9.

Large: Sk rnds 2, 3, and 4.

Ch 64 (72, 81), join first and last lps of ch with sl st. Mark beg of rnd. Rnds are worked continuously.

Rnd 1: Work 1 sc in each ch around.

Rnd 2: *Work 1 sc in next 6 sc, 2 sc in next sc*; rep from * to * 9 times—72 sc.

Rnds 3, 5, and 7: Work 1 sc in each sc around.

Rnd 4: *Work 1 sc in next 7 sc, 2 sc in next sc*; rep from * to * 9 times—81 sc.

Rnd 6: *Work 1 sc in next 8 sc, 2 sc in next sc*; rep from * to * 9 times—90 sc.

Rnd 8: *Work 1 sc in next 9 sc, 2 sc in next sc*; rep from * to * 9 times—99 sc.

Rnd 9: Work 1 sc in each sc around. Finish off.

ASSEMBLY

With WS of top and bottom together, join pieces by working sc in each sc around outside edge. Finish off.

FINISHING

Trim

Work 1 sc in each sc around bottom inside edge of headband. Work 3 more rows of sc around. Finish off.

Bubbles

With color B, make 13 bubbles, using beret top instructions as indicated.

- Make 4, following rnds 1–3.
- Make 3, following rnds 1–5.
- Make 4, following rnds 1–7.
- Make 2, following rnds 1–9.

Sew bubbles to pullover and beret randomly (see photo). Placement does not need to be exact.

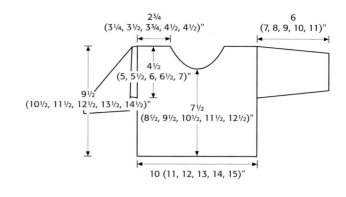

2¾
(3¼, 3½, 3¾, 4½, 4½)"

6
(7, 8, 9, 10, 11)"

4½
(5, 5½, 6, 6½, 7)"

9½
(10½, 11½, 12½, 13½, 14½)"

7½
(8½, 9½, 10½, 11½, 12½)"

10 (11, 12, 13, 14, 15)"

Beret

17 (19, 21)"

Carefree Days Cardigan and Shorts

Seed stitching, patch pockets, and vibrant colors make this adorable suit a little boy's favorite.

SIZES

Cardigan: 6–12M (18M, 24M, 2T, 3T, 4T)

Finished Chest Measurement: 20 (22, 24, 26, 28, 30)"

Shorts: 6–12M (18M, 24M, 2T, 3T, 4T)

Waist Measurement: 16 (17, 18, 19, 20, 21)"

MATERIALS

A 4 (4, 5, 6, 7, 7) balls Plymouth Wildflower DK (50g, 137yds/ball; 51% cotton, 49% acrylic), Navy 60

B 1 ball Plymouth Wildflower DK, Bright Yellow 48

C 1 ball Plymouth Wildflower DK, Aqua Blue 55

Size 5.5 mm (I/9 US) crochet hook or size needed to obtain gauge

1 yd. of ¾"-wide elastic band

5 (5, 5, 5, 6, 6) buttons, ½" diameter

GAUGE

16 sts and 20 rows = 4" in sc

CARDIGAN

BACK

With color A, ch 48 (52, 56, 60, 64, 68).

Row 1: Work 1 sc in second ch from hook, *ch 1, sk next ch, sc in next ch*; rep from * to * across, ch 1, turn—47 (51, 55, 59, 63, 67) sts.

Row 2: Work 1 sc in first sc, 1 sc in first ch-1 sp, *ch 1, sk next sc, work 1 sc in next ch-1 sp*; rep from * to * across, work 1 sc in last sc, ch 1, turn.

Row 3: Work 1 sc in first sc, ch 1, *sk next sc, work 1 sc in next ch-1 sp, ch 1*; rep from * to * across to last 2 sc, sk next sc, work 1 sc in last sc, ch 1, turn.

Rep rows 2 and 3 until back measures 9 (10, 11, 12, 13, 14)" from beg. Finish off.

FRONT (Make 2)

With color A, ch 24 (26, 28, 30, 32, 34).

Row 1: Work 1 sc in second ch from hook, *ch 1, sk next ch, work 1 sc in next ch*; rep from * to * across, ch 1, turn—23 (25, 27, 29, 31, 33) sts.

Row 2: Work 1 sc in first sc, 1 sc in first ch-1 sp, *ch 1, sk next sc, work 1 sc in next ch-1 sp*; rep from * to * across, work 1 sc in last sc, ch 1, turn.

Row 3: Work 1 sc in first sc, ch 1, *sk next sc, work 1 sc in next ch-1 sp, ch 1*; rep from * to * across to last 2 sc, sk next sc, work 1 sc in last sc, ch 1, turn.

Rep rows 2 and 3 until front measures 9 (10, 11, 12, 13, 14)" from beg. Finish off.

SLEEVES (Make 2)
With color A, ch 20 (22, 22, 24, 24, 26).

Row 1: Work 1 sc in second ch from hook, *ch 1, sk next ch, work 1 sc in next ch*; rep from * to * across, ch 1, turn—19 (21, 21, 23, 23, 25) sts.

Row 2: Work 1 sc in first sc, 1 sc in first ch-1 sp, *ch 1, sk next sc, work 1 sc in next ch-1 sp*; rep from * to * across, work 1 sc in last sc, ch 1, turn.

Row 3: Work 1 sc in first sc, ch 1, *sk next sc, work 1 sc in next ch-1 sp, ch 1*; rep from * to * across to last 2 sc, sk next sc, work 1 sc in last sc, ch 1, turn.

Rep rows 2 and 3 until sleeve measures 1½ (2, 2, 2½, 2½ , 3)" from beg. Finish off.

POCKETS (Make 2)
Make 1 with color B, 1 with color C.

Ch 10 (10, 11, 12, 13, 14).

Row 1: Work 1 sc in second ch from hook and in each ch across, ch 1, turn—9 (9, 10, 11, 12, 13) sc.

Row 2: Work 1 sc in each sc across, ch 1, turn.

Rep row 2 another 9 (9, 10, 11, 12, 13) times. Finish off.

ASSEMBLY
Join shoulders: With RS of front and back together, sew 2½ (3, 3½, 4, 4, 4½)" from outside edge on each shoulder. Attach sleeves: Measure down 4 (4½, 4½, 5, 5, 5½)" from shoulder seam on front and back and place markers. Sew in sleeves between markers. Sew side and underarm seams.

FINISHING
Trim

With color B, work 2 rows sc evenly around left sleeve edge. Finish off.

With color C, work 2 rows sc evenly around right sleeve edge. Finish off.

Pockets

Center pocket in lower one-third of front. Sew color B pocket to right front, color C pocket to left front.

Front Placket (buttonhole side)

Row 1: With color A, attach yarn to top edge and evenly work 28 (32, 34, 34, 39, 39) sc down front edge, ch 1, turn.

Row 2: Work 1 sc in next 1 (1, 2, 2, 1, 1) sc, ch 2, sk next 2 sc, *work 1 sc in next 4 (5, 5, 5, 5, 5) sc, ch 2, sk next 2 sc*; rep from * to * another 3 (3, 3, 3, 4, 4) times, work 1 sc in last 1 (1, 2, 2, 1, 1) sc, ch 1, turn.

Row 3: Work 1 sc in each sc and 2 sc in each ch-2 sp across, ch 1, turn.

Row 4: Work 1 sc in each sc across. Finish off.

Front Placket (button side)

Row 1: With color A, attach yarn to top edge and evenly work 28 (32, 34, 34, 39, 39) sc down front edge, ch 1, turn.

Row 2: Work 1 sc in each sc across, ch 1, turn.

Rep row 2 another 2 times. Finish off.

Attach buttons to correspond with buttonholes.

Collar

Row 1: With color B, attach yarn to top edge and evenly work 42 (46, 50, 52, 54, 56) sc around neck edge (including top edge of placket), ch 1, turn.

Row 2: Work 1 sc in each sc across, ch 1, turn.

Rep row 2 another 6 (6, 8, 8, 10, 10) times. Finish off.

SHORTS

SIDES (Make 2)

With color A, ch 54 (56, 58, 60, 62, 64).

Row 1: Work 1 sc in second ch from hook, *ch 1, sk next ch, work 1 sc in next ch*; rep from * to *across, ch 1, turn—53 (55, 57, 59, 61, 63) sts.

Row 2: Work 1 sc in first sc, 1 sc in first ch-1 sp, *ch 1, sk next sc, work 1 sc in next ch-1 sp*; rep from * to * across, work 1 sc in last sc, ch 1, turn.

Row 3: Work 1 sc in first sc, ch 1, *sk next sc, work 1 sc in next ch-1 sp, ch 1*; rep from * to * across to last 2 sc, sk next sc, work 1 sc in last sc, ch 1, turn.

Rep rows 2 and 3 until side measures 1½ (1½, 2, 2, 2½ , 2½)" from beg. Do not finish off.

LEG SHAPING

Dec 2 sts at beg and end of row for next 3 rows—41 (43, 45, 47, 49, 51) sts.

Cont working patt until side measures 7½ (7½, 9, 9, 10, 10)" from beg. Finish off.

ASSEMBLY

With RS facing, sew center seams of front and back, then st inside leg seams.

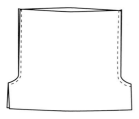

Sew front to back.

Sew inside leg seams.

FINISHING

Trim

With color C, work 2 rows sc evenly around edge of left leg. Finish off. With color B, work 2 rows sc evenly around edge of right leg. Finish off.

Waistband

With color C, attach yarn to top of shorts.

Rnd 1: Work 1 sc in each st around.

Rep rnd 1 another 11 times. Finish off.

To make casing, fold waistband down around outside edge. Sew seams, leaving an opening to insert elastic. Cut elastic 16½ (17½, 18½, 19½, 20½, 21½)" long. Insert elastic through casing. Lap ends ½" and sew together. Sew opening in casing closed.

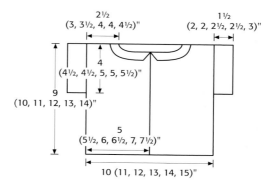

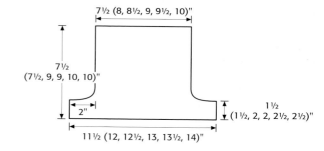

PREPPY PULLOVER AND POCKETBOOK

Harvard? Princeton? Well, maybe preschool. She'll be looking the part in a bright pink pullover accented with green flowers and trim. A matching pocketbook completes the ensemble.

SIZES

Pullover: 6–12M (18M, 24M, 2T, 3T, 4T)

Finished Chest Measurement: 20 (22, 24, 26, 28, 30)"

Pocketbook: 7" x 4½"

MATERIALS

A 4 (4, 5, 6, 7, 8) balls Plymouth Wildflower DK (50g, 137yds/ball; 51% cotton, 49% acrylic), Fuchsia 59

B 2 (2, 2, 2, 2, 3) balls Plymouth Wildflower DK, Lime 58

Size 5.5 (I/9 US) mm crochet hook (for pullover and flowers)

Size 6.0 (J/10 US) mm crochet hook (for pocketbook)

GAUGE

Sweater and Flowers: 16 sts and 20 rows = 4" in sc

Pocketbook: 14 sts and 16 rows = 4" using 2 strands of yarn in sc

PULLOVER

BACK

With color A, ch 41 (45, 49, 53, 57, 61).

Row 1: Work 1 sc in second ch from hook and in each ch across, ch 1, turn—40 (44, 48, 52, 56, 60) sc.

Row 2: Work 1 sc in each sc across, ch 1, turn.

Rep row 2 until back measures 9½ (10½, 11½, 12½, 13½, 14½)" from beg. Finish off.

FRONT

Work as for back until front measures 7½ (8½, 9½, 10½, 11½, 12½)" from beg. Beg neck shaping.

NECK SHAPING

Work both sides at same time.

Row 1: Work 1 sc in first 15 (17, 19, 20, 22, 24) sc, sk next 10 (10, 10, 12, 12, 12) sc; with a second ball of yarn, work 1 sc in rem 15 (17, 19, 20, 22, 24) sc.

Next 4 (4, 4, 5, 5, 5) rows: Work across each row, dec 1 sc at neck edge—11 (13, 15, 15, 17, 19) sc rem on each side.

All rem rows: Work 1 sc in each sc across, ch 1, turn. Rep until front measures 9½ (10½, 11½, 12½, 13½, 14½)" from beg. Finish off.

SLEEVES (Make 2)

With color A, ch 25 (27, 29, 31, 33, 35).

Row 1: Work 1 sc in second ch from hook and in each sc across, ch 1, turn—24 (26, 28, 30, 32, 34) sc.

Rows 2, 3, and 4: Work 1 sc in each sc across, ch 1, turn.

Row 5: Work 2 sc in first sc, 1 sc in each sc across, 2 sc in last sc, ch 1, turn.

Rep rows 1–5 until sleeve measures 6 (7, 8, 9, 10, 11)" from beg—36 (40, 44, 48, 52, 56) sc. Finish off.

ASSEMBLY

Join shoulders: With RS of front and back together, sew 2¾ (3¼, 3½, 3¾, 4½, 4½)" from outside edge on each shoulder. Attach sleeves: Measure down 4½ (5, 5½, 6, 6½, 7)" from shoulder seam on front and back and place markers. Sew in sleeves between markers. Sew side and underarm seams.

FINISHING

Trim

With color A, work 2 rows sc evenly around neck edge. With color B, sc around edges of neck, sleeves, and bottom edge of pullover.

Flowers

Make 8 flowers, 2 with color A and 6 with color B.

Ch 2.

Rnd 1: Work 5 sc in second ch from hook.

Rnd 2: Work (1 sc, ch 2, 2 dc, ch 2, 1 sc) in first sc; rep in each sc—5 petals. Finish off.

Measure 2" up from bottom and place 3 markers evenly across front. Center flowers over markers and sew. Rep for back.

POCKETBOOK

Use 2 strands and a 6.0 mm crochet hook for all parts except flowers.

SIDES (Make 2)

With color B, ch 14.

Row 1: Work 1 sc in second ch from hook and in each ch across, ch 1, turn—13 sc.

Next 13 rows: Work 1 sc in each sc across, ch 1, turn. Finish off.

FRONT AND BACK

With color B, ch 22.

Row 1: Work 1 sc in second ch from hook and in each ch across, ch 1, turn—21 sc.

Next 13 rows: Work 1 sc in each sc across, ch 1, turn. Finish off.

Rep to make back.

BOTTOM

With color B, ch 22.

Row 1: Work 1 sc in second ch from hook and in each ch across, ch 1, turn—21 sc.

Next 14 rows: Work 1 sc in each sc across, ch 1, turn. Finish off.

HANDLES (Make 2)

With color A, ch 3.

Row 1: Work 1 sc in second ch from hook and in each ch across, ch 1, turn.

Row 2: Work 1 sc in each sc across, ch 1, turn—2 sc.

Rep row 2 until handle measures 12". Finish off.

Sc around outside edges.

ASSEMBLY

With RS facing out, sc sides to front and back on outside edge. Attach bottom to lower edges of pocketbook with sc around outside edge. Measure and place markers 2" from outside edges of front and back. Center handles over markers and sew in place.

FINISHING

Center flowers on front and back and sew into place. Measure 1" from top corners on front, back, and sides and place markers. Sew between marker and edge.

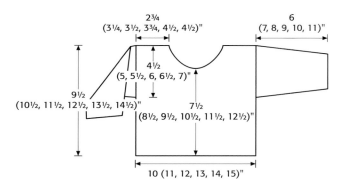

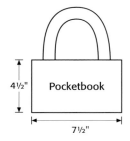

SUGAR 'N' SPICE CARDIGAN

Perfect for a boy or girl, this denim basket-weave cardigan has brick-colored accents on the collar and cuffs. Hand-painted gingerbread-man buttons complete this sweet treat!

SIZES

Cardigan: 6–12M (18–24M, 2T, 3T, 4T)

Finished Chest Measurement: 20 (23, 26, 28, 30)"

MATERIALS

A 4 (5, 6, 7, 8) balls Plymouth Wildflower DK (50g, 137yds/ball; 51% cotton, 49% acrylic), Denim Blue 10

B 1 ball Plymouth Wildflower DK, Brick 12

Size 5.5 mm (I/9 US) crochet hook or size needed to obtain gauge

5 (5, 5, 6, 6) buttons, 5/8" diameter

GAUGE

16 sts and 20 rows = 4" in sc

CARDIGAN

BACK

With color A, ch 46 (52, 58, 64, 70).

Row 1: Work 1 dc in fourth ch from hook and in each ch across, ch 2 (counts as first st on next row, now and throughout), turn—44 (50, 56, 62, 68) dc.

Row 2: Sk first dc, *work 1 FPdc around each of next 3 dc, 1 BPdc around each of next 3 dc*; rep from * to * across, work 1 hdc in top of beg ch, ch 2, turn.

Row 3: Sk first hdc, *work 1 FPdc around next 3 sts, 1 BPdc around next 3 sts*; rep from * to * across, work 1 hdc in top of beg ch, ch 2, turn.

Row 4: Sk first hdc, *work 1 BPdc around next 3 sts, 1 FPdc around next 3 sts*; rep from * to * across, work 1 hdc in top of beg ch, ch 2, turn.

Row 5: Rep row 4.

Row 6: Rep row 3.

Rep rows 3–6 until back measures 9½ (10½, 11½, 12½, 13½)" from beg. Finish off.

FRONT (Make 2)

With color A, ch 22 (28, 28, 34, 34).

Row 1: Work 1 dc in fourth ch from hook and in each ch across, ch 2 (counts as first st on next row, now and throughout), turn—20 (26, 26, 32, 32) dc.

Row 2: Sk first dc, *work 1 FPdc around each of next 3 dc, 1 BPdc around each of next 3 dc*; rep from * to * across, work 1 hdc in top of beg ch, ch 2, turn.

Row 3: Sk first hdc, *work 1 FPdc around next 3 sts, 1 BPdc around next 3 sts*; rep from * to * across, work 1 hdc in top of beg ch, ch 2, turn.

Row 4: Sk first hdc, *work BPdc around next 3 sts, work FPdc around next 3 sts*; rep from * to * across, work 1 hdc in top of beg ch, ch 2, turn.

Row 5: Rep row 4.

Row 6: Rep row 3.

Rep rows 3–6 until front measures 9½ (10½, 11½, 12½, 13½)" from beg. Finish off.

SLEEVES (Make 2)
With color A, ch 40 (46, 46, 52, 52).

Row 1: Work 1 dc in fourth ch from hook and in each ch across, ch 2 (counts as first st on next row, now and throughout), turn—38 (44, 44, 50, 50) dc.

Row 2: Sk first dc, *work 1 FPdc around each of next 3 dc, 1 BPdc around each of next 3 dc*; rep from * to * across, work 1 hdc in top of beg ch, ch 2, turn.

Row 3: Sk first hdc, *work 1 FPdc around next 3 sts, 1 BPdc around next 3 sts*; rep from * to * across, work 1 hdc in top of beg ch, ch 2, turn.

Row 4: Sk first hdc, *work 1 BPdc around next 3 sts, 1 FPdc around next 3 sts*; rep from * to * across, work 1 hdc in top of beg ch, ch 2, turn.

Row 5: Rep row 4.

Row 6: Rep row 3.

Rep rows 3–6 until sleeve measures 5½ (6½, 7½, 8½, 9½)" from beg. Finish off.

ASSEMBLY
With RS of front and back together, sew 2½ (3, 3½, 4, 4½)" from outside edge on each shoulder. Measure down 4½ (5, 5, 5½, 5½)" from shoulder seam on front and back and place markers. Sew in sleeves between markers. Sew side and underarm seams.

FINISHING
Front Placket (buttonhole side)
Row 1: With color A, attach yarn to top edge and evenly work 28 (32, 34, 39, 39) sc down front edge, ch 1, turn.

Row 2: Work 1 sc in next 1(1, 2, 1, 1) sc, ch 2, sk next 2 sc, *work 1 sc in next 4 (5, 5, 5, 5) sc, ch 2, sk next 2 sc*; rep from * to * another 3 (3, 3, 4, 4) times, work 1 sc in last 1(1, 2, 1, 1) sc in row, ch 1, turn.

Row 3: Work 1 sc in each sc and 2 sc in each ch-2 sp across, ch 1, turn.

Row 4: Work 1 sc in each sc across. Finish off.

Front Placket (button side)
Row 1: With color A, attach yarn to top edge and evenly work 28 (32, 34, 39, 39) sc down front edge, ch 1, turn.

Row 2: Work 1 sc in each sc across, ch 1, turn.

Rep row 2 another 2 times. Finish off.

Attach buttons, using buttonholes as spacing guides.

Collar
Row 1: With color B, attach yarn to top edge and evenly work 42 (46, 50, 52, 54) sc around neck edge (including top edge of placket), ch 1, turn.

Row 2: Work 1 sc in each sc across, ch 1, turn.

Rep row 2 another 6 (8, 8, 10, 10) times. Finish off.

Cuffs
Rnd 1: With color B, work 36 (42, 42, 48, 48) sc evenly around cuff.

Rnd 2: Dec 1 sc over next 2 sc as follows: *insert hook into next st, yo, draw up lp (2 lps on hook), insert hook into next st, yo and draw up lp (3 lps on hook), yo and draw through all 3 lps on hook*; rep from * to * around.

Next 3 rnds: Work 1 sc in each sc around. Finish off.

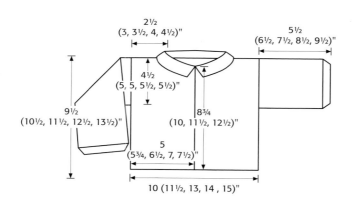

NORDIC TWIST PULLOVER AND BEANIE

Hit the slopes in this sweater and beanie. Wide bands of texture stitching on cuffs, waistband, stand-up collar, and beanie give this outfit its Nordic flair.

SKILL LEVEL: INTERMEDIATE

SIZES

Pullover: 6–12M (18M, 24M, 2T, 3T, 4T)

Finished Chest Measurement: 20 (22, 24, 26, 28, 30)"

Beanie: Small (Medium, Large)

Circumference: 16 (18, 20)"

MATERIALS

A 1 ball Plymouth Wildflower DK (50g, 137yds/ball; 51% cotton, 49% acrylic), Purple 45

B 4 (4, 5, 6, 7, 8) balls Plymouth Wildflower DK, Periwinkle 74

C 1 ball Plymouth Wildflower DK, Saffron 78

Size 5.5 mm (I/9 US) crochet hook or size needed to obtain gauge

GAUGE

16 sts and 20 rows = 4" in sc

PULLOVER

FRONT AND BACK

With color A, ch 43 (47, 51, 55, 59, 63).

Row 1: Work 1 sc in second ch from hook and in each ch across. Change to B, ch 1, turn—42 (46, 50, 54, 58, 62) sc.

Row 2: Work 1 sc in each sc across, ch 1, turn.

Row 3: Work 1 sc in each sc across. Change to color C, ch 1, turn.

Note: FPdc is worked around next st on second or third row below (as instructed). Always sk the st on the working row behind the FPdc.

Row 4: Work 1 sc in first 2 sc on working row; 1 FPdc around each of next 2 sc on third row below, 1 sc in next 2 sc on working row, *1 FPdc around each of next 2 sc on third row below, 1 sc in next 2 sc on working row*; rep from * to * across, ch 1, turn.

Row 5: Work 1 sc in each sc and in each FPdc across. Change to color A, ch 1, turn.

Rows 6, 8, 10, and 12: Work 1 sc in first 2 sc, *1 FPdc around each of next 2 FPdc on second row below; 1 sc in next 2 sc on working row*; rep from * to * across, ch 1, turn.

Row 7: Work 1 sc in each sc and FPdc across. Change to color B, ch 1, turn.

Row 9: Work 1 sc in each sc and FPdc across. Change to color C, ch 1, turn.

Row 11: Work 1 sc in each sc and FPdc across. Change to color A, ch 1, turn.

Row 13: Work 1 sc in each sc and FPdc across. Change to color B, ch 1, turn.

Row 14: Work 1 sc in each sc in back lp only across, ch 1, turn.

Row 15: Work 1 sc in each sc across, ch 1, turn.

Rep row 15 until front measures 10 (11, 12, 13, 14, 15)" from beg. Finish off. Rep to make back.

SLEEVES (Make 2)
With color A, ch 31 (31, 35, 35, 39, 39).

Row 1: Work 1 sc in second ch from hook and in each ch across. Change to color B, ch 1, turn—30 (30, 34, 34, 38, 38) sc.

Row 2: Work 1 sc in each sc across, ch 1, turn.

Row 3: Work 1 sc in each sc across. Change to color C, ch 1, turn.

Row 4: Work 1 sc in first 2 sc on working row, 1 FPdc in each of next 2 sc on third row below, 1 sc in next 2 sc on working row, *1 FPdc in each of next 2 sc on third row below, 1 sc in next 2 sc on working row*; rep from * to * across, ch 1, turn.

Row 5: Work 1 sc in each sc and in each FPdc across. Change to color A, ch 1, turn.

Rows 6, 8, 10, and 12: Work 1 sc in first 2 sc, *1 FPdc around each of next 2 FPdc on second row below, 1 sc in next 2 sc on working row*; rep from * to * across, ch 1, turn.

Row 7: Work 1 sc in each sc and FPdc across. Change to color B, ch 1, turn.

Row 9: Work 1 sc in each sc and FPdc across. Change to color C, ch 1, turn.

Row 11: Work 1 sc in each sc and FPdc across. Change to color A, ch 1, turn.

Row 13: Work 1 sc in each sc and FPdc across. Change to color B, ch 1, turn.

Row 14: Work 1 sc in each sc in back lp only across, ch 1, turn.

Row 15: Work 1 sc in each sc across, ch 1, turn.

Row 16: Work 2 sc in first sc, 1 sc in each sc across, 2 sc in last sc, ch 1, turn.

*Next 5 (7, 8, 10, 12, 13) rows: Work 1 sc in each sc across, ch 1, turn.

Next row: Work 2 sc in first sc, 1 sc in each sc across, 2 sc in last sc, ch 1, turn*; rep from * to * another 2 times. Sleeve measures 6 (7, 8, 9, 10, 11)" from beg. Finish off.

ASSEMBLY
Join shoulders: With RS of front and back together, sew 1¾ (2, 2¼, 2½, 2¾, 3)" from outside edge on each shoulder. Attach sleeves: Measure down 4¾ (4¾, 5¼, 5¼, 5¾, 5¾)" from shoulder seam on back and front and place markers. Sew in sleeves between markers. Sew side and underarm seams.

FINISHING
Collar
With color A, attach yarn to neck edge.

Rnd 1: Work 52 (56, 60, 64, 68, 72) sc evenly around neck edge, join with sl st to first sc. Change to color B, ch 1, turn.

Rnd 2: Work 1 sc in each sc across, join with sl st to first st, ch 1, turn.

Rnd 3: Work 1 sc in each sc across, join with sl st to first st. Change to color C, ch 1, turn.

Rnd 4: Work 1 sc in first 2 sc on working row; 1 FPdc around each of next 2 sc on third row below (be sure to work these sts on outside of garment), 1 sc in next 2 sc on working row, *1 FPdc around each of next 2 sc on third row below, 1 sc in next 2 sc on working row*; rep from * to * across, join with sl st to first st, ch 1, turn.

Rnd 5: Work 1 sc in each sc and FPdc across, join with sl st to first st. Change to color A, ch 1, turn.

Rnd 6: Work 1 sc in first 2 sc, *1 FPdc around each of next 2 FPdc on second row below, 1 sc in next 2 sc on working row*; rep from * to * across, join with sl st to first st, ch 1, turn.

Rnd 7: Work 1 sc in each sc and FPdc across, join with sl st to first st. Finish off.

BEANIE

Small: Sk rnds 18–26.

Medium: Sk rnds 21–24.

Large: Complete all rnds.

Note: Turn only as indicated at end of rnds. Work all other rnds continuously, placing a marker at the beg of each rnd.

With color A, ch 64 (72, 80), join with sl st to first st, ch 1, turn.

Rnd 1: Work 1 sc in second ch from hook and in each ch across. Change to color B, join with sl st to first st, ch 1, turn.

Rnd 2: Work 1 sc in each sc across, join with sl st to first st, ch 1, turn.

Rnd 3: Work 1 sc in each sc across. Change to color C, join with sl st to first st, ch 1, turn.

Rnd 4: Work 1 sc in first 2 sc on working row, 1 FPdc around each of next 2 sc on third row below, 1 sc in next 2 sc on working row, *1 FPdc around each of next 2 sc on third row below, 1 sc in next 2 sc on working row*; rep from * to * across, join with sl st to first st, ch 1, turn.

Rnd 5: Work 1 sc in each sc and FPdc across. Change to color A, join with sl st to first st, ch 1, turn.

Rnds 6, 8, 10, and 12: Work 1 sc in first 2 sc, *1 FPdc around each of next 2 FPdc on second row below, 1 sc in next 2 sc on working row*; rep from * to * across, join with sl st to first st, ch 1, turn.

Rnd 7: Work 1 sc in each sc and FPdc across. Change to color B, join with sl st to first st, ch 1, turn.

Rnd 9: Work 1 sc in each sc and FPdc across. Change to color C, join with sl st to first st, ch 1, turn.

Rnd 11: Work 1 sc in each sc and FPdc across. Change to color A, join with sl st to first st, ch 1, turn.

Rnd 13: Work 1 sc in each sc and FPdc across. Change to color B, join with sl st to first st, ch 1, turn.

Rnd 14: Work 1 sc in back lp only of each sc across, join with sl st to first st, ch 1, turn.

Rnds 15–22: Work 1 sc in each sc around.

Rnd 23: *Work 1 sc in first 18 sc, dec 1 sc over next 2 sc*; rep from * to * around—76 sc.

Rnds 24–40: *Work 1 sc in first 17 sc, dec 1 sc over next 2 sc*; rep from * to * 4 times—72 sc. Cont to work rnds, dec number of sc you work in by 1 for each of the 4 repeats within each rnd. You will dec total number of sc by 4 on each rnd—8 sc at end of rnd 40.

Rnd 41: *Dec 1 sc over next 2 sc*; rep from * to * around—4 sc.

Rnd 42: *Dec 1 sc over next 2 sc*; rep from * to * around—2 sc. Finish off.

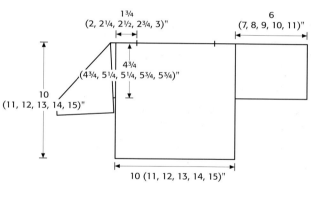

Beanie

16 (18, 20)"

POPSICLE HAT
AND SCARF

The whimsical colors of this Popsicle hat and scarf will brighten up the dreariest of days. This texture-stitched set makes a perfect "quick-crochet" gift.

SKILL LEVEL: ADVANCED BEGINNER

SIZES

Hat: Small (Medium, Large)

Circumference: 16 (17½, 19)"

Scarf: 6" x 32"

MATERIALS

A 1 (1, 2) balls Plymouth Wildflower DK (50g, 137yds/ball; 51% cotton, 49% acrylic), Aqua Blue 55

B 10 yards Plymouth Wildflower DK, Yellow 48

C 2 (3, 3) balls Plymouth Wildflower DK, Lime Green 58

D 1 ball Plymouth Wildflower DK, Orange 56

Size 5.5 mm (I/9 US) crochet hook or size needed to obtain gauge

Pom-pom maker

GAUGE

16 sts and 20 rows = 4" in sc

PATTERN STITCH

Bubble stitch: Yo, insert hook into next st, *yo, draw lp through, yo, draw through 2 lps*; rep from * to * another 4 times, yo, draw through 6 lps.

HAT

With color A, ch 60 (66, 72). Join with sl st to first ch in row to form a circle.

Rnd 1: Work 1 sc in second ch from hook and in each ch around. Join with sl st to first sc, ch 1, turn—60 (66, 72) sc.

Rnd 2: *Work 1 bubble st in next sc, 1 sc in next 2 sc*; rep from * to * around. Join with sl st to first st in rnd, ch 1, turn.

Rnds 3, 5, and 7: Work 1 sc in each sc around. Join with sl st to first st in rnd, ch 1, turn.

Rnd 4: *Work 1 sc in next 2 sc, 1 bubble st in next sc*; rep from * to * around. Join with sl st to first st in rnd, ch 1, turn.

Rnd 6: *Work 1 bubble st in next sc, 1 sc in next 2 sc*; rep from * to * around. Join with sl st to first st in rnd, ch 1, turn.

Rnd 8: *Work 1 sc in next 2 sc, 1 bubble st in next sc*; rep from * to * around. Join with sl st to first st in rnd, ch 1, turn.

Rnd 9: Work 1 sc in each sc around. Join with sl st to first st in rnd. Change to color B, ch 1, turn.

Rnd 10: Work 1 sc in each sc around to last sc, 2 sc in last sc. Join with sl st to first st in rnd. Change to color C, ch 1, turn.

Rnd 11: Work 1 sc in each sc around in back lps only. Join with sl st to first st in rnd, ch 1, turn.

Rnd 12: *Work 1 sc and 2 dc in next sc, sk next 2 sc*; rep from * to * around, work 1 sc in last sc. Join with sl st to first st in rnd, ch 1, turn.

Rep rnd 12 until hat measures 7 (8, 8½)" from beg. Finish off. Cut a 12"-long piece of color C. Weave yarn through each st in last row. Pull ends of yarn tightly and tie a knot.

FINISHING

With approximately 10 yds of color D, make a 1½" pom-pom and attach to top of hat. With color D, work 1 row of sc evenly around hat bottom. Next row: Sl st in each sc around. Finish off.

SCARF

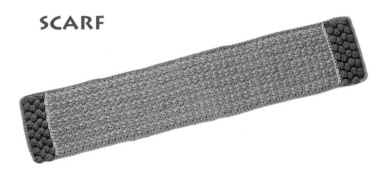

With color A, ch 22. Join with sl st to first ch in row to from a circle. Beg bubble-st border.

Row 1: Work 1 sc in second ch from hook and in each ch across, ch 1, turn—21 sc.

Row 2: *Work 1 bubble st in next sc, 1 sc in next 2 sc*; rep from * to * across, ch 1, turn.

Rows 3, 5, and 7: Work 1 sc in each sc across, ch 1, turn.

Row 4: *Work 1 sc in next 2 sc, 1 bubble st in next sc*; rep from * to * across, ch 1, turn.

Row 6: *Work 1 bubble st in next sc, 1 sc in next 2 sc*; rep from * to * across, ch 1, turn.

Row 8: *Work 1 sc in next 2 sc, 1 bubble st in next sc*; rep from * to * across, ch 1, turn.

Row 9: Work 1 sc in each sc across. Change to color B, ch 1, turn.

Row 10: Work 1 sc in each sc across to last sc, 2 sc in last sc. Change to color C, ch 1, turn.

Row 11: Work 1 sc in each sc across in back lps only, ch 1, turn.

Row 12: *Work 1 sc and 2 dc in next sc, sk next 2 sc*; rep from * to * across, ch 1, turn.

Rep row 12 until scarf measures 29" from beg.

Change to color B and beg bubble-st border.

Row 1: Work 1 sc in each sc across. Change to color A, ch 1, turn.

Row 2: Work 1 sc in each sc across in back lps only, ch 1, turn.

Row 3: *Work 1 bubble st in next sc, 1 sc in next 2 sc*; rep from * to * across, ch 1, turn.

Rows 4 and 6: Work 1 sc in each sc across, ch 1, turn.

Row 5: *Work 1 sc in next 2 sc, 1 bubble st in next sc*; rep from * to * across, ch 1, turn.

Row 7: *Work 1 bubble st in next sc, 1 sc in next 2 sc*; rep from * to * across, ch 1, turn.

Row 8: Work 1 sc in each sc across. Finish off.

FINISHING

With color D, work 1 row sc evenly around outside edges; work 3 sc in each corner. Next row: Sl st in each sc around. Finish off.

32"   Scarf

6"

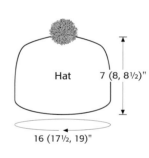

Hat   7 (8, 8½)"

16 (17½, 19)"

BIBLIOGRAPHY

These are a few of my favorite books. They serve as great inspiration as well as handy reference tools.

Bonnette, Mary H. and Jo Lynne Murchland. *Paintbox Knits: More Than 30 Designs for Kids.* Woodinville, Wash.: Martingale & Company, 2001.

Carr, Sandy, Josie May, and Eleanor Van Zandt. *Knitting: A Step-by-Step Guide.* New York: Portland House, 1990.

Carroll, Amy, ed., and Dorthea Hall, contributor. *The Pattern Library Crochet.* London: Ebury Press, National Magazine House, 1981.

Diven, Gail and Cindy Kitchel. *The Complete Idiot's Guide to Knitting and Crocheting.* New York: Macmillan Publishing, 1999.

Huxley, Susan. *Crocheted Sweaters: Simple Stitches, Great Designs.* Woodinville, Wash.: Martingale & Company, 2001.

Leinhauser, Jean. *101 Crochet Stitches.* San Marcos, Calif.: ASN Publishing, 1995.

———. *101 Crochet Stitches for Afghans.* San Marcos, Calif.: ASN Publishing, 1996.

Sims, Darla. *63 Easy-to-Crochet Pattern Stitches.* Little Rock, Ark.: Leisure Arts, Inc., 1987.

Toth, Cecilia. *Good Houskeeping: The Illustrated Guide to Needlecrafts.* New York: Hearst Books, 1994.

ACKNOWLEDGMENTS

This book would not have been possible without the help of many generous and talented people. I would like to offer a special thanks to the following:

The staff of Martingale & Company. (Added thanks to my technical editor, Ursula Reikes.)

Models: Sarah Bradley, April Bradley, Hadley Queen, Mackenzie Meyers, Ryan Meyers, Anjali Bose, Devan Bose, Wren Sablich, Elizabeth Hussin, and Jack Costello. (A special thanks to each one of their parents!)

Photographer: John Hamel

Sample Garment Construction: Virginia Robertson

Yarn: Plymouth Yarn Company

ABOUT THE AUTHOR

Nancy Queen is an avid crocheter and designer with almost 20 years of experience in the fashion merchandising, design, and garment industries. Inspired by the birth of her daughter, she now designs and publishes worldwide a collection of children's crochet patterns that are whimsical, fun, and easy to make.

Under her labels Nancy Queen Designs (www.nancyqueendesigns.com) and NobleKnits (www.nobleknits.com), Nancy also designs and produces crochet kits, patterns, and instructional tools. She has produced a bestselling video, *Crochet Basics Instructional Video.* She has appeared on QVC with a line designed exclusively for the shopping network. Her work has been featured in *Vogue Knitting* magazine, *Family Circle Easy Knitting* magazine, Interweave Press's *Knit Notes,* and *Crochet!* magazine.

Nancy is a member of the Crochet Guild of America, the National Needlework Association, and the Hobby Industry Association. She and her family live in Valley Forge, Pennsylvania, where she continues to enjoy designing new patterns and kits.

new and bestselling titles from

America's Best-Loved Craft & Hobby Books®

America's Best-Loved Quilt Books®

NEW RELEASES
1000 Great Quilt Blocks
Basically Brilliant Knits
Bright Quilts from Down Under
Christmas Delights
Creative Machine Stitching
Crochet for Tots
Crocheted Aran Sweaters
Cutting Corners
Everyday Embellishments
Folk Art Friends
Garden Party
Hocus Pocus!
Just Can't Cut It!
Quilter's Home: Winter, The
Sweet and Simple Baby Quilts
Time to Quilt
Today's Crochet
Traditional Quilts to Paper Piece

APPLIQUÉ
Appliquilt in the Cabin
Artful Album Quilts
Artful Appliqué
Blossoms in Winter
Color-Blend Appliqué
Sunbonnet Sue All through the Year

BABY QUILTS
Easy Paper-Pieced Baby Quilts
Even More Quilts for Baby
More Quilts for Baby
Play Quilts
Quilted Nursery, The
Quilts for Baby

HOLIDAY QUILTS & CRAFTS
Christmas Cats and Dogs
Creepy Crafty Halloween
Handcrafted Christmas, A
Make Room for Christmas Quilts
Welcome to the North Pole

HOME DECORATING
Decorated Kitchen, The
Decorated Porch, The
Dresden Fan
Gracing the Table
Make Room for Quilts
Quilts for Mantels and More
Sweet Dreams

LEARNING TO QUILT
101 Fabulous Rotary-Cut Quilts
Beyond the Blocks
Casual Quilter, The
Feathers That Fly
Joy of Quilting, The
Simple Joys of Quilting, The
Your First Quilt Book (or it should be!)

PAPER PIECING
40 Bright and Bold Paper-Pieced Blocks
50 Fabulous Paper-Pieced Stars
For the Birds
Quilter's Ark, A
Rich Traditions
Split-Diamond Dazzlers

ROTARY CUTTING
365 Quilt Blocks a Year Perpetual Calendar
Around the Block Again
Around the Block with Judy Hopkins
Fat Quarter Quilts
More Fat Quarter Quilts
Stack the Deck!
Triangle Tricks
Triangle-Free Quilts

SCRAP QUILTS
Nickel Quilts
Scrap Frenzy
Scrappy Duos
Spectacular Scraps
Strips and Strings
Successful Scrap Quilts

TOPICS IN QUILTMAKING
American Stenciled Quilts
Americana Quilts
Batik Beauties
Bed and Breakfast Quilts
Fabulous Quilts from Favorite Patterns
Frayed-Edge Fun
Patriotic Little Quilts
Reversible Quilts

CRAFTS
ABCs of Making Teddy Bears, The
Blissful Bath, The
Handcrafted Frames
Handcrafted Garden Accents
Handprint Quilts
Painted Chairs
Painted Whimsies

KNITTING & CROCHET
365 Knitting Stitches a Year Perpetual
   Calendar
Clever Knits
Crochet for Babies and Toddlers
Crocheted Sweaters
Knitted Sweaters for Every Season
Knitted Throws and More
Knitter's Book of Finishing Techniques, The
Knitter's Template, A
More Paintbox Knits
Paintbox Knits
Too Cute! Cotton Knits for Toddlers
Treasury of Rowan Knits, A
Ultimate Knitter's Guide, The

Our books are available at bookstores and your favorite craft, fabric, and yarn retailers. If you don't see the title you're looking for, visit us at **www.martingale-pub.com** or contact us at:

1-800-426-3126

International: 1-425-483-3313

Fax: 1-425-486-7596

Email: info@martingale-pub.com

For more information and a full list of our titles, visit our Web site.